HEADLINE SE

No. 318   FOREIGN POLICY ASSOCIATION   Winter 1998

...And Justice for All:

The Universal Declaration
of Human Rights at 50

Cover Design: Ed Bohon $10.95

Special Issue

*In honor of the 50th anniversary of
the Universal Declaration of Human Rights,
the Foreign Policy Association and the Great Books
Foundation present for reading and discussion the
following compilation of relevant excerpted articles and
texts, together with pertinent questions.*

The Foreign Policy Association

The Foreign Policy Association is a private, nonprofit, nonpartisan educational organization. Its purpose is to stimulate wider interest and more effective participation in, and greater understanding of, world affairs among American citizens. Among its activities is the continuous publication, dating from 1935, of the HEADLINE SERIES.

HEADLINE SERIES (ISSN 0017-8780) is published four times a year, Spring, Summer, Fall and Winter, by the Foreign Policy Association, Inc., 470 Park Avenue So., New York, NY 10016. Chairman, Paul B. Ford; President, Noel V. Lateef; Editor in Chief, Karen M. Rohan; Managing Editor, Ann R. Monjo; Associate Editor, Nicholas Barratt; Editorial Assistant, Agnes Kostro. Subscription rates, $20.00 for 4 issues; $35.00 for 8 issues; $50.00 for 12 issues. Single copy price $5.95; double issue $11.25; special issue $10.95. Discount 25% on 10 to 99 copies; 30% on 100 to 499; 35% on 500 and over. Payment must accompany all orders. Postage and handling: $2.50 for first copy; $.50 each additional copy. Second-class postage paid at New York, NY, and additional mailing offices. POSTMASTER: Send address changes to HEADLINE SERIES, Foreign Policy Association, 470 Park Avenue So., New York, NY 10016. Copyright 1998 by Foreign Policy Association, Inc. Design by K.M. Rohan. Printed at Science Press, Ephrata, Pennsylvania. Published Winter 1998.

Library of Congress Catalog Card No. 98-73867
ISBN 0-87124-187-0

Foreword

On the 50th anniversary of the Universal Declaration of Human Rights, a model for constitutions the world over, the Foreign Policy Association and the Great Books Foundation are pleased to cooperate on a special HEADLINE SERIES that reviews the evolution of human rights and their role in U.S. foreign policy.

One of the great concerns in 1948 was outlawing genocide. Cambodia, Bosnia and Rwanda are reminders that the battle has not been won. People's darkest impulses, born of avarice, ignorance and prejudice, continue to manifest themselves in willful acts of barbarism and oppression. What role, therefore, should human rights play in U.S. foreign policy?

For Jimmy Carter, human rights are "the soul of American foreign policy." Critics respond that a foreign policy based on human rights is doomed to failure because it emphasizes principle, values and morality instead of pragmatism, national interest and power. In relations with many countries, the U.S. government faces increasing pressure to decide what priority it will assign human rights.

The universality of human rights is perhaps the most unambiguous message of the Universal Declaration. This message was recently underscored by United Nations Secretary General Kofi Annan: "Human rights are African rights. They are also Asian rights; they are European rights; they are American rights. They belong to no government, they are limited to no continent, for they are fundamental to humankind itself."

As we approach the new millennium, what challenge could be more noble than the promotion of human dignity through the widest possible adherence to basic norms of human decency?

3

The Human Rights Idea*
by Louis Henkin

THE CONTEMPORARY idea of human rights was formulated and given content during the Second World War and its aftermath. During the War, the Allied powers had proclaimed that assuring respect for human rights was their war aim. In 1945, at Nuremberg, the Allies included crimes against humanity among the charges on which Nazi leaders were tried. The United Nations Charter declared that promoting respect for human rights was a principal purpose of the United Nations Organization. The human rights idea found its contemporary expression in the Universal Declaration of Human Rights adopted by the United Nations General Assembly in 1948, and in the numerous covenants and conventions derived from it.

"Rights" have figured prominently in moral, legal, and po-

In keeping with the format of the HEADLINE SERIES, the Foreign Policy Association begins this volume with an essay presenting the views of a prominent scholar on a topic of contemporary foreign policy. Dr. Henkin's essay provides one set of answers to some of the questions about the Universal Declaration of Human Rights raised later in this volume by the Great Books Foundation. It is our hope that by giving careful consideration to this and the other readings that follow, readers will further their own thinking on this critical set of issues.

*From *The Age of Rights*, by Louis Henkin ©1990 Columbia University Press. Reprinted with the permission of the publisher.

litical theory. The idea of rights is related to theories of "the good," of "the right," of "justice," and to conceptions of "the good society." In contemporary philosophical literature the idea of rights is often considered an alternative to various brands of utilitarianism.

Individual rights as a political idea draws on natural law and its offspring, natural rights. In its modern manifestation that idea is traced to John Locke, to famous articulations in the American Declaration of Independence and in the French Declaration of the Rights of Man and of the Citizen, and to realizations of the idea in the United States Constitution and its Bill of Rights and in the constitutions and laws of modern states.

The idea of human rights that has received currency and universal (if nominal) acceptance in our day owes much to these antecedents, but it is discrete and different from them. The contemporary version does not ground or justify itself in natural law, in social contract, or in any other political theory. In international instruments representatives of states declare and recognize human rights, define their content, and ordain their consequences within political societies and in the system of nation-states. The justification of human rights is rhetorical, not philosophical. Human rights are self-evident, implied in other ideas that are commonly intuited and accepted. Human rights are derived from accepted principles, or are required by accepted ends—societal ends such as peace and justice; individual ends such as human dignity, happiness, fulfillment.

What the pattern of declared norms amounts to, the idea it reflects, is nowhere articulated. I attempt to do so here, not as a philosophical construct, but as a distillation of what underlies national and international instruments.

Human rights are rights of individuals in society. Every human being has, or is entitled to have, "rights"—legitimate, valid, justified claims—upon his or her society; claims to various "goods" and benefits. Human rights are not some abstract, inchoate "good"; they are defined, particular claims listed in international instruments such as the Universal Declaration of Human Rights and the major covenants and conventions. They are those benefits deemed essential for individual well-being, dignity, and fulfillment, and that reflect a common sense of justice, fairness, and decency. In the constitutional jurisprudence of the United States, as we shall see, individual rights have long been thought of as consisting only of "immunities," as limitations on what government might do to the individual. Human rights, on the other hand, include not only these negative "immunity claims" but also positive "resource claims," claims to what society is deemed required to do *for* the individual. They include liberties— freedom *from* (for example, detention, torture), and freedom *to* (speak, assemble); they include also the right to food, housing, and other basic human needs.

Human rights are universal: they belong to every human being in every human society. They do not differ with geography or history, culture or ideology, political or economic system, or stage of societal development. To call them "human" implies that all human beings have them, equally and in equal measure, by virtue of their humanity—regardless of sex, race, age; regardless of high or low "birth," social class, national origin, ethnic or tribal affiliation; regardless of wealth or poverty, occupation, talent, merit, religion, ideology, or other commitment. Implied in one's humanity, human rights are inalienable and imprescriptible: they cannot be transferred, forfeited, or waived; they cannot be lost by having been usurped, or by one's failure to exercise or assert them.

Human rights are *rights*; they are not merely aspirations, or assertions of the good. To call them rights is not to assert, merely, that the benefits indicated are desirable or necessary; or, merely, that it is "right" that the individual shall enjoy these goods; or even, merely, that it is the duty of society to respect the immunity or provide the benefits. To call them "rights" implies that they are claims "as of right," not by appeal to grace, or charity, or brotherhood, or love; they need not be earned or deserved. The idea of rights implies entitlement on the part or the holder in some order under some applicable norm; the idea of human rights implies entitlement in a moral order under a moral law, to be translated into and confirmed as legal entitlement in the legal order of a political society. When a society recognizes that a person has a right, it affirms, legitimates, and justifies that entitlement, and incorporates and establishes it in the society's system of values, giving it important weight in competition with other societal values.

Human rights imply the obligation of society to satisfy those claims. The state must develop institutions and procedures, must plan, must mobilize resources as necessary to meet those claims. Political and civil rights require laws, institutions, procedures, and other safeguards against tyranny, against corrupt, immoral, and inefficient agencies or officials. Economic and social rights in modern society require taxation and spending and a network of agencies for social welfare. The idea of human rights implies also that society must provide some system of remedies to which individuals may resort to obtain the benefits to which they are entitled or be compensated for their loss. Together, the affirmation of entitlement, the recognition by society of an obligation to mobilize itself to discharge it, and the implication of remedy, all enhance the likelihood that the right will be realized, that individuals will actually enjoy the benefits to which they are entitled.

Human rights are claims upon society. These claims may derive from moral principles governing relations between persons, but it is society that bears the obligation to satisfy the claims. Of course, the official representatives of society must themselves respect individual freedoms and immunities; political society must also act to protect the individual's rights against private invasion. As regards claims to economic and social benefits, society must act as insurer to provide them if individuals cannot provide them for themselves. Thus, government must protect me from assault by my neighbor, or from wolves, and must ensure that I have bread or hospitalization; in human rights terms my rights are against the state, not against the neighbor or the wolves, the baker, or the hospital. The state may arrange to satisfy my claims by maintaining domestic laws and institutions that give me, say, rights and remedies in tort against my neighbor, or administrative remedies against a corrupt, misguided, or inefficient bureaucrat, or access to public schools or health services. Those legal rights and remedies against individuals or agencies within society give effect to my human rights claims upon society.

The idea of human rights has implications for the relation of the individual's rights to other public goods. It is commonly said that human rights are "fundamental." That means that they are important, that life, dignity, and other important human values depend on them; it does not mean that they are "absolute," that they may never be abridged for any purpose in any circumstances. Human rights enjoy a prima facie, presumptive inviolability, and will often "trump" other public goods. Government may not do some things, and must do others, even though the authorities are persuaded that it is in the society's interest (and perhaps even in the individual's own interest) to do otherwise; individual human rights cannot be lightly sacrificed even for the good of the greatest number, even for the general good of all. But if human rights do not bow lightly to public concerns, they may be sacrificed if countervailing societal interests are important enough, in particular circumstances, for limited times and purposes, to the extent strictly necessary. The Universal Declaration recognizes that rights are subject to limitations determined by law "for the purpose of securing due recognition and respect for the rights and freedoms of others and of meeting the just requirements of morality, public order, and the general welfare in a democratic society."

The idea of rights accepts that some limitations on rights are permissible but the limitations are themselves strictly limited. Public emergency, national security, public order are weighty terms, bespeaking important societal interests, but they are not to be lightly or loosely invoked, and the conception of national security or public order cannot be so large as to swallow the right. Derogations are permitted only in time of a public emergency that threatens the life of the nation, not as a response to fears (warranted or paranoid) for other values, or for the security of a particular regime. Even in an authentic emergency, a society may derogate from rights only to the extent strictly required by the exigencies of the situation, and even such necessary derogations must not involve invidious inequalities, and may not derogate from basic rights: they must not invade the right to life, or involve torture or cruel, inhuman punishment, slavery or servitude, conviction of crime under *ex post facto* laws, denial of rights as a person before the law, or violate freedom of thought, conscience, or religion. Moreover, considerations of public emergency permitting derogations, or of national security or public order permitting limitations on certain rights, refer to a universal standard, monitored by external scrutiny and judgment.

In sum, the idea of human rights is that the individual counts—independent of and in addition to his or her part in the common good. Autonomy and liberty must be respected, and the individual's basic economic-social needs realized, as a matter of entitlement, not of grace or discretion (even by wise and benevolent authority, or even by "the people"). The individual has obligations to others and to the community, and society may ask all individuals to give up some of their rights for the rights of others and for the common good, but there is a core of individuality that cannot be invaded or sacrificed. And all individuals count equally. An individual's right can be sacrificed to another's right only when choice is inevitable, and only according to some principle of choice reflecting the comparative value of each right. No particular individual can be singled out for particular sacrifice, except at random or by some other "neutral principle," consistent with the spirit of equal protection of the laws.

I have referred to rights as claims upon society, not *against* society. In the ideology of rights, human rights are not "against society," against the interest of society; on the contrary, the good society is one in which individual rights flourish, and the promotion and protection of every individual's rights are a public good. There is an aura of conflict between individual and society only in that individual rights are asserted against government, against those who represent society officially, and because the human rights idea often requires that an individual's right be preferred to some other public good. But this apparent conflict between individual and society is specious; in the longer, deeper view, the society is better if the individual's rights are respected.

Human rights, as conceived by and specified in the Universal Declaration and other international instruments, are the rights of individuals. They include the individual's right to associate with others and to form groups of varying character for various purposes. The individual has the right to marry and create a family, to join a religious community and to pursue religious, cultural, or social activities with them, to identify with an ethnic or other group and to pursue their common interests, to join a political party or trade union. But the essential human rights idea addresses the rights of the individual, not of any group or collectivity.

Groups may have rights in domestic legal systems but, at least at its origin, the human rights movement did not address them. Later, the principal international human rights covenants declared the rights of "peoples" to self-determination and to sovereignty over their natural resources, but those provisions were an exceptional addition to the general conception in the covenants that human rights are claims of a person upon his or her own society. There has been a movement to recognize other "generations of rights"—a right to peace, to development, to a healthy environment— but none of these has been incorporated into any legally binding human rights agreement.

Political and Moral Underpinnings

The idea of rights here distilled from contemporary international instruments responds, I believe, to common moral intuitions and accepted political principles. Those intuitions and principles have not been authoritatively articulated. Developed during the decades following the Second World War, international human rights are not the work of philosophers, but of politicians and citizens, and philosophers have only begun to try to build conceptual justifications for them. The international expressions of rights themselves claim no philosophical foundation, nor do they reflect any clear philosophical assumptions; they articulate no particular moral principles or any single, comprehensive theory of the relation of the individual to society. That there are "fundamental human rights" was a declared article of faith, "reaffirmed" by "the peoples of the United Nations" in the United Nations Charter. The Universal Declaration of Human Rights, striving for a pronouncement that would appeal to diverse political systems governing diverse peoples, built on that faith and shunned philosophical exploration. Because of that faith—and of political and ideological forces—governments accepted the concept of human rights, agreed that they were properly matters for international concern, cooperated to define them, assumed international obligations to respect them, and submitted to some international scrutiny as to their compliance with these obligations.

International human rights derive from natural rights theories and systems, harking back through English, American, and French constitutionalism to John Locke et al., and earlier natural rights and natural law theory. In its American version, that constitutionalism included concepts of original individual autonomy translated into popular sovereignty; of a social compact providing for continued self-government through accountable representatives; or limited government for limited purposes; and retained, inalienable, individual rights. But the profound influence of that constitutionalism on international acceptance of human rights did not depend on, or take with it, commitment to all the underlying theory. International human rights reflect no comprehensive political theory of the relation of individual to society, only what is implied in the idea of individual rights against society. Human Rights are "inherent" but not necessarily "retained" from any hypothetical state of nature anteceding government. There is a nod to popular sovereignty, but nothing of social compact or of continuing consent of the governed. Retained rights are not the condition of government, and violating them does not necessarily give rise to a right to undo government by revolution. Inevitably, international human rights also implicate the purposes for which governments are created, but they surely do not imply a commitment to government for limited purposes only. Born after various forms of socialism were established and spreading, and commitment to welfare economics and the welfare state was nearly universal, international human rights implied rather a conception of government as designed for all purposes and seasons. The rights deemed to be fundamental included not only limitations precluding government from invading civil and political rights, but positive obligations for government to promote economic and social well-being, implying government that is activist, intervening, planning, committed to economic-social programs for the society that would translate into economic-social rights for the individual.

Those who built international human rights perhaps saw these rights as "natural," but in a contemporary sense; human rights correspond to the nature of human beings and of human society, to his or her psychology and its sociology. Rights (to quote from the principal international instruments) "derive from the inherent dignity of the human person." "Recognition . . . of the equal and inalienable rights of all members of the human family is the foundation of freedom, justice and peace in the world." Respect for, and observance of, human rights will help create "conditions of stability and well-being which are necessary for peaceful and friendly relations among nations." We are not told what theory justifies "human dignity" as the source of rights, or how human dignity is defined or its needs determined. We are not told what conception of justice is reflected in human rights, or how preserving human rights will promote peace in the world.

Necessarily, however, the idea of rights reflected in the instruments, the particular rights recognized, and the consequent responsibilities for political societies, imply particular political ideas and moral principles. International human rights does not hint at any theory of social contract, but it is committed to popular sovereignty. "The will of the people shall be the basis of the authority of government" and is to "be expressed in periodic and genuine elections which shall be by universal and equal suffrage." It is not required that government based on the will of the people take any particular form. Presumably, Western-style presidential or parliamentary systems and communist "democratic centralism" might both be equally consistent with the international standard—provided the people in fact have control over how they are governed, provided they have the freedom and the means to inform their governors of their wishes, provided the governors are accountable in fact and the people can replace them at frequent, regular intervals. In any system, government by bureaucracy is presumably not government by the people if, although political authority is conceived and couched in legal forms and decorated with occasional formal votes, arbitrary power in fact prevails, without meaningful accountability and meaningful opportunity for the people to terminate or control the exercise of such power. The will of the people is not the basis of the authority of government if the people are not free to change their form of government or their political and economic system, for instance, to move toward—or away from—socialism or a market economy.

International human rights has no commitment to any particular economic system, and a society is free to choose between a market economy and socialism and among the various gradations and combinations of each. Some of the human rights recognized, however, imply commitment to some political-economic principles. Every person has a right to own property and not to be arbitrarily deprived of it; the right to work and be free to choose employment; to enjoy trade union protection against a powerful employer, private or public; and to be protected against unemployment or its consequences.

International human rights imply a broad conception of the purposes and responsibilities of government. The obligation of society to ensure rights may require government to plan, to regulate, to tax and to spend. Perhaps civil and political rights can be respected—in a fortunate society—by a civilized citizenry, and a minimal, honest, and benign officialdom, without any special societal interventions. But if citizen civility and official self-restraint are insufficient, the society must intervene, by civil rights acts and other laws, by institutions and remedies governing the behavior of citizen and official. Economic and social rights (food, shelter, work, health, and education) can perhaps be secured—in a fortunate society—by private initiative and means, by market forces, by employment contracts, by private insurance. But society must ensure these rights, must act as "insurer" for them; it must do what is necessary to see that such rights are in fact enjoyed, whether by improving the performance of private agencies or by supplementing or replacing these efforts by official programs.

Beneath the responsibilities of government for individual rights are political principles governing the relation of the individual to political authority, and beneath those political principles appear to be moral principles governing relations between individual human beings. If government responds to the will of the governed, the undertaking by governments to respect and ensure individual rights implies that the governed recognize these rights for each of them, and assume responsibility for these rights even when other interests, including other common interests, compete. The individual must recognize the obligation, both as an individual and as a member of the sovereign people (the majority), to respect and ensure those rights, to support the laws and institutions and the costs necessary to make the agreed-upon rights secure.

Political-moral principles are implied both in the idea of rights and in the particular rights recognized. Of course, a commitment to fair trial in the criminal process reflects a common sense of justice requiring that a person—not only I, but any other person—not be found guilty and deprived of freedom if he or she is innocent. Political-moral principles are implied in the fact that individuals not only demand for themselves, but also recognize for others equally, the autonomy, the physical integrity and freedom, the rights to due process, to property, to privacy, to "personhood," to liberties, as well as to basic human needs and other economic and social rights.

Less obvious are the moral assumptions underlying the other dispositions of the idea of rights. In general, what government may not do are those things we may not do to each other, and the reason why officials may not do them—say, deprive us of our life, liberty, privacy, or property—is because ordinarily no individual may do that to another. Human dignity requires respect from my neighbor as well as from the state. Under the international instruments the state is required not only to respect but to ensure rights, that is, ensure respect for them by private persons. By what moral calculus, then, are officials permitted to do to an individual what his neighbor may not?

Implicit political-moral principles accept limitations on individual rights for the common good—to protect society against external enemies and internal disorder, or to regulate individual activity for the benefit of others and for the common welfare. Therefore, the state is permitted to take away my freedom through the criminal law, at least when imprisonment is designed to prevent and rehabilitate, probably also if it aims to deter, and perhaps even when the purpose is to express moral judgment by societal retribution. It is permissible to take away my property through taxation in order to provide for the common defense and the public welfare. From some perspectives at least, it may be assumed that these limitations on the individual are acceptable because the individual consents to them, or consented to them, in principle and in advance, by living in society and thereby submitting to government by democratic process. Individuals consent *a priori*, it can be argued, even to the possibility that they might be sent to their deaths for the common cause, on the assumption, or hope, that the need will not arise, and the sacrifice not prove necessary; that if someone will have to be sacrificed it will be someone else; that others submit to the same risk for one's own welfare, and that the selection will be by lot or chance or at least according to some rational, neutral principle. Whether such consent to the sacrifice of one's rights is authentic, whether an individual is really free to leave society so that his or her continuing consent can be assumed, is debatable and may differ from society to society, time to time, context to context, individual to individual. Or, perhaps—without insisting on consent and contract as the basis for rights and for limitations on rights—limitations on individual liberty or property are to be justified on notions of equity and practicability and some uncertain blend of the rights idea with utilitarian dedication to the "general welfare" or to maximum total happiness.

The commitment in the human rights idea to the welfare society may imply other political-moral principles or assumptions. It implies, I think, that the basic human needs of those unable to provide for themselves are the responsibility of all, and that it is permissible if not obligatory to take from those who have (as by taxation) to provide for those who have not. Such moral obligation has been supported on various grounds:

- In the twentieth century, societies and political institutions are created and maintained for broad purposes; not only for security against one's neighbor and against external aggression, but to assure the welfare of all and each.

The social contract includes agreement to create a welfare state.

- In a society with a complex, integrated economy, the economically disadvantaged—for example, the unemployed—are victims of deficiencies in the economic system, often of policies that purposefully maintain such disadvantages for systemic ends. Those who benefit from the system are therefore morally obligated to help those who suffer from it, at least to the extent of assuring their basic human needs.
- We are all members of a community that benefits all. Community and communality imply obligations, and high among them is the obligation to assure basic human needs for those who cannot satisfy their own.
- We have moved away from the moral intuitions of the Anglo-Saxon tradition which saw the Good Samaritan as acting from charity, not from moral obligation. Today, we are coming to believe, one is morally obligated to save a person in danger, at least if it can be done without undue risk or cost to oneself. There is, then, a moral obligation for one who can, to save another from death or serious injury, as by starvation. If, in the case of the hungry in the community, that obligation is indeterminate in that the moral obligation to save any one person does not ordinarily attach to any other particular person, it attaches to all members of the community collectively. The collective obligation can be met by any collective action but effectively falls on the political authorities of society to meet by public action with public funds.

The moral foundations for human rights within society apply to all societies, and perhaps also between societies, as economies and polities become interdependent and community and communality expand. The idea of human rights, born in the West, has spread and, nominally at least, been universally accepted. Sovereign states continue to resist, but the implementation of the human rights idea has been "internationalized," and become the concern of the international community of states.

...And Justice for All:
Readings for Discussion from the
Great Books Foundation
Selected and edited by Mark A. Cwik

Introduction

THERE ARE MANY WAYS to think and talk about the Universal Declaration of Human Rights (UDHR). Discussion can address the circumstances from which the declaration arose and the impact that it has had; the debates that were involved in its formulation; the status of the UDHR as an international document; the possibility and the practicalities of gaining world-wide adherence to its standards. Such discussion will ask questions that are historical, political, legal and perhaps economic.

Another way to talk about the Universal Declaration of Human Rights, one so obvious that it might be taken for granted, is to simply explore the ideas presented by the words of the document itself. A discussion of this kind asks questions that are *interpretive*, questions that pursue basic meaning. The reading selections and questions in the following pages have been chosen to help foster this type of inquiry.

The text of the Universal Declaration of Human Rights is presented along with ten writings that deal with issues of rights, justice, law and equality. These selections and the questions accompanying them are intended to illuminate many of the basic concepts embodied in the UDHR and to aid in a discussion of its strengths and its weaknesses.

About These Readings

The title *And Justice for All* carries with it an implicit comparison of the rights proclaimed in the UDHR with those in the tradition of rights that has evolved in the United States. The U.S. Declaration of Independence and Bill of Rights, together with the French Declaration of the Rights of Man and the Citizen, serve as important examples of statements of rights that preceded the Universal Declaration of Human Rights, and, thus, are natural companion texts to the UDHR.

The seven subsequent readings span the late seventeenth to late twentieth centuries. Each of these selections serves to highlight one or more major facets of the Universal Declaration of Human Rights; each also stands on its own as worthy of close reading and discussion. They address issues that, fifty years after the proclamation of the UDHR, remain unresolved.

Shared Inquiry Discussion

While the works in this collection can serve as the basis of profitable individual reading and reflection about the Universal Declaration of Human Rights, they have been specially cho sen with an eye toward their use in group discussion.

The Great Books Foundation promotes a specific discussion approach called Shared Inquiry. In Shared Inquiry discussion, participants search for answers to fundamental questions raised by a text. This search is inherently active, taking what the author has written and trying to grasp its full meaning, to interpret or reach an understanding of the text in light of personal experience and with the aid of sound reasoning.

Shared Inquiry provides an especially appropriate method

for an honest exchange of ideas on the Universal Declaration of Human Rights. The process of truly open discussion challenges participants to listen to the views of others and to face the possibility of changing their own. And the respectful airing and testing of ideas in discussion ultimately leads to clearer and deeper thinking on a subject as complex as the UDHR.

The Great Books Foundation teaches the Shared Inquiry method in hundreds of workshops throughout the country each year, but any discussion group can benefit from what the Foundation has learned in fifty years of promoting high-quality discussion on serious and challenging topics. The Great Books Foundation has found that this interpretive type of discussion will be more focused and fruitful if

- All participants have read the selection carefully before discussion, preferably twice
- Discussion stays centered on the selection everyone has read
- Participants can support their opinions with evidence from the reading selection
- The discussion leader asks only genuine and open questions and seeks not to teach, but to learn with, the group.

Discussion Questions

The questions that accompany each of the readings are intended to focus discussion on a search for an understanding of the words and ideas in each text. The questions are phrased to ask participants to approach a text on its own terms, before they pass judgment upon it. Of the many kinds of questions that are appropriate to ask of a text, these interpretive questions afford the most direct engagement between author and audience. It is assumed, and encouraged, that discussion participants will contribute their own questions in addition to those provided.

Beyond the questions specific to each selection, a number of more general, fundamental questions unite all of the readings in this *And Justice for All* book. They are questions that, taken together, form a framework for the entire collection:

- What are rights?
- Where do rights come from?
- How many rights are there and why is it necessary to enumerate them?
- Do rights change with time?
- What is a declaration and what is it intended to achieve?
- What is the relation between freedoms and rights?
- What is the difference between "civil" rights and "human" rights?
- For a right to exist, must it be recognized?
- Who or what are the enemies of rights?

These are questions that may never be completely resolved. What is important is that they continue to be considered and discussed.

Note to Readers: Many of the readings in this collection have been edited for length, in order to present as many different perspectives as possible.

Preamble to the Charter of the United Nations

Signed on June 26, 1945

We the peoples of the United Nations

determined

to save succeeding generations from the scourge of war, which twice in our lifetime has brought untold sorrow to mankind, and

to reaffirm faith in fundamental human rights, in the dignity and worth of the human person, in the equal rights of men and women and of nations large and small, and

to establish conditions under which justice and respect for the obligations arising from treaties and other sources of international law can be maintained, and

to promote social progress and better standards of life in larger freedom,

and for these ends

to practice tolerance and live together in peace with one another as good neighbors, and

to unite our strength to maintain international peace and security, and

to ensure, by the acceptance of principles and the institution of methods, that armed force shall not be used, save in the common interest, and

to employ international machinery for the promotion of the economic and social advancement of all peoples,

have resolved to combine our efforts
to accomplish these aims.

Accordingly, our respective Governments, through representatives assembled in the city of San Francisco, who have exhibited their full powers found to be in good and due form, have agreed to the present Charter of the United Nations and do hereby establish an international organization to be known as the United Nations.

Universal Declaration of Human Rights

Adopted without dissent December 10, 1948, by the General Assembly of the United Nations. (Forty-eight countries voted in favor of the resolution. Eight countries abstained: Byelorussian SSR, Czechoslovakia, Poland, Saudi Arabia, Ukrainian SSR, Union of South Africa, USSR, Yugoslavia.)

Preamble

Whereas recognition of the inherent dignity and of the equal and inalienable rights of all members of the human family is the foundation of freedom, justice and peace in the world,

Whereas disregard and contempt for human rights have resulted in barbarous acts which have outraged the conscience of mankind, and the advent of a world in which human beings shall enjoy freedom of speech and belief and freedom from fear and want has been proclaimed as the highest aspiration of the common people,

Whereas it is essential, if man is not to be compelled to have recourse, as a last resort, to rebellion against tyranny and oppression, that human rights should be protected by the rule of law,

Whereas it is essential to promote the development of friendly relations between nations,

Whereas the peoples of the United Nations have in the Charter reaffirmed their faith in fundamental human rights, in the dignity and worth of the human person and in the equal rights of men and women and have determined to promote social progress and better standards of life in larger freedom,

Whereas Member States have pledged themselves to achieve, in cooperation with the United Nations, the promotion of universal respect for and observance of human rights and fundamental freedoms,

Whereas a common understanding of these rights and freedoms is of the greatest importance for the full realization of this pledge,

Now, Therefore,
The General Assembly
proclaims
**This Universal Declaration
of Human Rights**

as a common standard of achievement for all peoples and all nations, to the end that every individual and every organ of society, keeping this Declaration constantly in mind, shall strive by teaching and education to promote respect for these rights and freedoms and by progressive measures, national and international, to secure their universal and effective recognition and observance, both among the peoples of Member States themselves and among the peoples of territories under their jurisdiction.

Article 1

All human beings are born free and equal in dignity and rights. They are endowed with reason and conscience and should act toward one another in a spirit of brotherhood.

Article 2

Everyone is entitled to all the rights and freedoms set forth in this Declaration, without distinction of any kind, such as race, color, sex, language, religion, political or other opinion, national or social origin, property, birth or other status. Furthermore, no distinction shall be made on the basis of the political, jurisdictional or international status of the country or territory to which a person belongs, whether it be independent, trust, non-self-governing or under any other limitation of sovereignty.

Article 3

Everyone has the right to life, liberty and security of person.

Article 4

No one shall be held in slavery or servitude; slavery and the slave trade shall be prohibited in all their forms.

Article 5

No one shall be subjected to torture or to cruel, inhuman or degrading treatment or punishment.

Article 6

Everyone has the right to recognition everywhere as a person before the law.

Article 7

All are equal before the law and are entitled without any discrimination to equal protection of the law. All are entitled to equal protection against any discrimination in violation of this Declaration and against any incitement to such discrimination.

Article 8

Everyone has the right to an effective remedy by the competent national tribunals for acts violating the fundamental rights granted him by the constitution or by law.

Article 9

No one shall be subjected to arbitrary arrest, detention or exile.

Article 10

Everyone is entitled in full equality to a fair and public hearing by an independent and impartial tribunal, in the determination of his rights and obligations and of any criminal charge against him.

Article 11

(1) Everyone charged with a penal offense has the right to be presumed innocent until proved guilty according to law in a public trial at which he has had all the guarantees necessary for his defense.

(2) No one shall be held guilty of any penal offense on account of any act or omission which did not constitute a penal offense, under national or international law, at the time when it was committed. Nor shall a heavier penalty be imposed than the one that was applicable at the time the penal offense was committed.

Article 12

No one shall be subjected to arbitrary interference with his privacy, family, home or correspondence, nor to attacks upon his honor and reputation. Everyone has the right to the protection of the law against such interference or attacks.

Article 13

(1) Everyone has the right to freedom of movement and residence within the borders of each State.

(2) Everyone has the right to leave any country, including his own, and to return to his country.

Article 14

(1) Everyone has the right to seek and to enjoy in other countries asylum from persecution.

(2) This right may not be invoked in the case of pros-

ecutions genuinely arising from nonpolitical crimes or from acts contrary to the purposes and principles of the United Nations.

Article 15

(1) Everyone has the right to a nationality.

(2) No one shall be arbitrarily deprived of his nationality nor denied the right to change his nationality.

Article 16

(1) Men and women of full age, without any limitation due to race, nationality or religion, have the right to marry and to found a family. They are entitled to equal rights as to marriage, during marriage and at its dissolution.

(2) Marriage shall be entered into only with the free and full consent of the intending spouses.

(3) The family is the natural and fundamental group unit of society and is entitled to protection by society and the State.

Article 17

(1) Everyone has the right to own property alone as well as in association with others.

(2) No one shall be arbitrarily deprived of his property.

Article 18

Everyone has the right to freedom of thought, conscience and religion; this right includes freedom to change his religion or belief, and freedom, either alone or in community with others and in public or private, to manifest his religion or belief in teaching, practice, worship and observance.

Article 19

Everyone has the right to freedom of opinion and expression; this right includes freedom to hold opinions without interference and to seek, receive and impart information and ideas through any media and regardless of frontiers.

Article 20

(1) Everyone has the right to freedom of peaceful assembly and association.

(2) No one may be compelled to belong to an association.

Article 21

(1) Everyone has the right to take part in the government of his country, directly or through freely chosen representatives.

(2) Everyone has the right to equal access to public service in his country.

(3) The will of the people shall be the basis of the authority of government; this will shall be expressed in periodic and genuine elections which shall be by universal and equal suffrage and shall be held by secret vote or by equivalent free voting procedures.

Article 22

Everyone, as a member of society, has the right to social security and is entitled to realization, through national effort and international cooperation and in accordance with the organization and resources of each State, of the economic, social and cultural rights indispensable for his dignity and the free development of his personality.

Article 23

(1) Everyone has the right to work, to free choice of employment, to just and favorable conditions of work and to protection against unemployment.

(2) Everyone, without any discrimination, has the right to equal pay for equal work.

(3) Everyone who works has the right to just and favorable remuneration ensuring for himself and his family an existence worthy of human dignity, and supplemented,

if necessary, by other means of social protection.

(4) Everyone has the right to form and to join trade unions for the protection of his interests.

Article 24

Everyone has the right to rest and leisure, including reasonable limitation of working hours and periodic holidays with pay.

Article 25

(1) Everyone has the right to a standard of living adequate for the health and well-being of himself and of his family, including food, clothing, housing and medical care and necessary social services, and the right to security in the event of unemployment, sickness, disability, widowhood, old age or other lack of livelihood in circumstances beyond his control.

(2) Motherhood and childhood are entitled to special care and assistance. All children, whether born in or out of wedlock, shall enjoy the same social protection.

Article 26

(1) Everyone has the right to education. Education shall be free, at least in the elementary and fundamental stages. Elementary education shall be compulsory. Technical and professional education shall be made generally available and higher education shall be equally accessible to all on the basis of merit.

(2) Education shall be directed to the full development of the human personality and to the strengthening of respect for human rights and fundamental freedoms. It shall promote understanding, tolerance and friendship among all nations, racial or religious groups, and shall further the activities of the United Nations for the maintenance of peace.

(3) Parents have a prior right to choose the kind of education that shall be given to their children.

Article 27

(1) Everyone has the right freely to participate in the cultural life of the community, to enjoy the arts and to share in scientific advancement and its benefits.

(2) Everyone has the right to the protection of the moral and material interests resulting from any scientific, literary or artistic production of which he is the author.

Article 28

Everyone is entitled to a social and international order in which the rights and freedoms set forth in this Declaration can be fully realized.

Article 29

(1) Everyone has duties to the community in which alone the free and full development of his personality is possible.

(2) In the exercise of his rights and freedoms, everyone shall be subject only to such limitations as are determined by law solely for the purpose of securing due recognition and respect for the rights and freedoms of others and of meeting the just requirements of morality, public order and the general welfare in a democratic society.

(3) These rights and freedoms may in no case be exercised contrary to the purposes and principles of the United Nations.

Article 30

Nothing in this Declaration may be interpreted as implying for any State, group or person any right to engage in any activity or to perform any act aimed at the destruction of any of the rights and freedoms set forth herein.

1. On what does the Universal Declaration of Human Rights (UDHR) base its belief in the "inherent dignity and . . . the equal and inalienable rights of all members of the human family"? (Preamble)

2. What is meant by "progressive measures" to secure the recognition and observance of the UDHR's rights and freedoms? (Preamble)

3. How does the UDHR accommodate the cultural, political, and religious traditions of different groups and nations? (Articles 16, 17, 18, 22, 26) What if a group's religious beliefs conflict with the UDHR?

4. Why does the UDHR provide for "special care and assistance" for motherhood and childhood? (Article 25)

5. What is meant by the "full development of the human personality"? (Article 26)

6. Does Article 28 oblige the international community to participate in the reform or overthrow of governments that do not respect, promote, protect or recognize these universal human rights?

7. Are there any rights that cannot justly be limited for the sake of the "general welfare"? (Article 29)

8. Does the UDHR favor any one system of government over any other?

9. Why does the UDHR put much less emphasis on duties than it does on rights?

10. Why does the UDHR call itself "universal"?

11. Which articles would you eliminate if you could? Why?

12. Is the entire document a statement of faith?

The Declaration of Independence

*In Congress, July 4, 1776. The unanimous Declaration
of the thirteen United States of America*

WHEN IN THE COURSE of human events, it becomes necessary for one people to dissolve the political bands which have connected them with another, and to assume among the powers of the earth, the separate and equal station to which the Laws of Nature and of Nature's God entitle them, a decent respect to the opinions of mankind requires that they should declare the causes which impel them to the separation.

We hold these truths to be self-evident, that all men are created equal, that they are endowed by their Creator with certain unalienable rights, that among these are life, liberty, and the pursuit of happiness. That to secure these rights, governments are instituted among men, deriving their just powers from the consent of the governed. That whenever any form of government becomes destructive of these ends, it is the right of the people to alter or to abolish it, and to institute new government, laying its foundation on such principles and organizing its powers in such form, as to them shall seem most likely to effect their safety and happiness. Prudence, indeed, will dictate that governments long established should not be changed for light and transient causes; and accordingly all experience hath shown, that mankind are more disposed to suffer, while evils are sufferable, than to right themselves by abolishing the forms to which they are accustomed. But when a long train of abuses and usurpations, pursuing invariably the same object evinces a design to reduce them under absolute despotism, it is their right, it is their duty, to throw off such government, and to provide new guards for their future security. Such has been the patient sufferance of these Colonies;

and such is now the necessity which constrains them to alter their former systems of government. The history of the present King of Great Britain is a history of repeated injuries and usurpations, all having in direct object the establishment of an absolute tyranny over these States. To prove this, let facts be submitted to a candid world.

He has refused his assent to laws, the most wholesome and necessary for the public good.

He has forbidden his Governors to pass laws of immediate and pressing importance, unless suspended in their operation till his assent should be obtained; and when so suspended, he has utterly neglected to attend to them.

He has refused to pass other laws for the accommodation of large districts of people, unless those people would relinquish the right of representation in the Legislature, a right inestimable to them and formidable to tyrants only.

He has called together legislative bodies at places unusual, uncomfortable, and distant from the depository of their public records, for the sole purpose of fatiguing them into compliance with his measures.

He has dissolved the representative houses repeatedly, for opposing with manly firmness his invasions on the rights of the people.

He has refused for a long time, after such dissolutions, to cause others to be elected; whereby the legislative powers, incapable of annihilation, have returned to the people at large for their exercise; the State remaining in the meantime exposed to all the danger of invasion from without and convulsions within.

He has endeavored to prevent the population of these states; for that purpose obstructing the laws of naturalization of foreigners; refusing to pass others to encourage their migration hither, and raising the conditions of new appropriations of lands.

He has obstructed the administration of justice, by refusing his assent to laws for establishing judiciary powers.

He has made judges dependent on his will alone, for the tenure of their offices, and the amount and payment of their salaries.

He has erected a multitude of new offices, and sent hither

swarms of officers to harass our people, and eat out their substance.

He has kept among us, in times of peace, standing armies without the consent of our legislatures.

He has affected to render the military independent of and superior to the civil power.

He has combined with others to subject us to a jurisdiction foreign to our constitution, and unacknowledged by our laws; giving his assent to their acts of pretended legislation:

For quartering large bodies of armed troops among us:

For protecting them, by a mock trial, from punishment for any murders which they should commit on the inhabitants of these States:

For cutting off our trade with all parts of the world:

For imposing taxes on us without our consent:

For depriving us in many cases, of the benefits of trial by jury:

For transporting us beyond seas to be tried for pretended offenses:

For abolishing the free system of English laws in a neighboring Province, establishing therein an arbitrary government, and enlarging its boundaries so as to render it at once an example and fit instrument for introducing the same absolute rule into these Colonies:

For taking away our Charters, abolishing our most valuable laws, and altering fundamentally the forms of our governments:

For suspending our own Legislatures, and declaring themselves invested with power to legislate for us in all cases whatsoever.

He has abdicated government here, by declaring us out of his protection and waging war against us.

He has plundered our seas, ravaged our coasts, burnt our towns, and destroyed the lives of our people.

He is at this time transporting large armies of foreign mercenaries to complete the works of death, desolation, and tyranny, already begun with circumstances of cruelty and perfidy scarcely paralleled in the most barbarous ages, and totally unworthy the head of a civilized nation.

He has constrained our fellow citizens taken captive on the high seas to bear arms against their country, to become the executioners of their friends and brethren, or to fall themselves by their hands.

He has excited domestic insurrections amongst us, and has endeavored to bring on the inhabitants of our frontiers, the merciless Indian savages, whose known rule of warfare is an undistinguished destruction of all ages, sexes, and conditions.

In every stage of these oppressions we have petitioned for redress in the most humble terms: our repeated petitions have been answered only by repeated injury. A prince whose character is thus marked by every act which may define a tyrant is unfit to be the ruler of a free people.

Nor have we been wanting in attention to our British brethren. We have warned them from time to time of attempts by their legislature to extend an unwarrantable jurisdiction over us. We have reminded them of the circumstances of our emigration and settlement here. We have appealed to their native justice and magnanimity, and we have conjured them by the ties of our common kindred to disavow these usurpations, which would inevitably interrupt our connections and correspondence. They too have been deaf to the voice of justice and consanguinity. We must, therefore, acquiesce in the necessity, which denounces our separation, and hold them, as we hold the rest of mankind, enemies in war, in peace friends.

WE, THEREFORE, the Representatives of the UNITED STATES OF AMERICA, in General Congress assembled, appealing to the Supreme Judge of the world for the rectitude of our intentions, do, in the name, and by the authority of the good people of these Colonies, solemnly publish and declare, That these United Colonies are, and of right ought to be FREE and INDEPENDENT STATES; that they are absolved from all allegiance to the British Crown, and that all political connection between them and the State of Great Britain, is and ought to be totally dissolved; and that as Free and Independent States, they have full power to levy war, conclude peace, contract alliances, establish commerce, and to do all other acts and things which Independent States may of right do. And for the support of this declaration, with a firm reliance on the protection of Divine Providence, we mutually pledge to each other our lives, our fortunes, and our sacred honor.

1. Why do the signers of the Declaration state that it is not only their right but their *duty* to change their government?

2. Why do the signers refer to "the Laws of Nature *and* of Nature's God"(italics added)?

3. Why do the signers say, "We hold these truths to be self-evident," and not say simply, "These truths are self-evident"?

4. Why do the signers of the Declaration proclaim that the equality of all men is "self-evident" and their rights "unalienable"?

5. Where do the signers think the right to overthrow a despotic government comes from?

6. Why do the colonists feel a need to proclaim to the world their reasons for declaring independence?

The Constitution
of the United States
Preamble and Bill of Rights

WE THE PEOPLE OF THE UNITED STATES, in order to form a more perfect Union, establish justice, insure domestic tranquility, provide for the common defense, promote the general welfare, and secure the blessings of liberty to ourselves and our posterity, do ordain and establish this Constitution for the United States of America.

Constitutional Amendments

Amendment 1

Congress shall make no law respecting an establishment of religion, or prohibiting the free exercise thereof; or abridging the freedom of speech, or of the press; or the right of the people peaceably to assemble, and to petition the Government for a redress of grievances.

Amendment 2

A well-regulated militia, being necessary to the security of a free State, the right of the people to keep and bear arms, shall not be infringed.

Amendment 3

No soldier shall, in time of peace be quartered in any house, without the consent of the owner, nor in time of war, but in a manner to be prescribed by law.

Amendment 4

The right of the people to be secure in their persons, houses, papers, and effects, against unreasonable searches and seizures, shall not be violated, and no warrants shall issue, but upon probable cause, supported by oath or affirmation, and particularly describing the place to be searched, and the persons or things to be seized.

Amendment 5

No person shall be held to answer for a capital, or otherwise infamous crime, unless on a presentment or indictment of a grand jury, except in cases arising in the land or naval forces, or in the militia, when in actual service in time of war or public danger; nor shall any person be subject for the same offense to be twice put in jeopardy of life or limb; nor shall be compelled in any criminal case to be a witness against himself, nor be deprived of life, liberty, or property, without due process of law; nor shall private property be taken for public use without just compensation.

Amendment 6

In all criminal prosecutions, the accused shall enjoy the right to a speedy and public trial, by an impartial jury of the State and district wherein the crime shall have been committed, which district shall have been previously ascertained by law, and to be informed of the nature and cause of the accusation; to be confronted with the witnesses against him; to have compulsory process for obtaining witnesses in his favor, and to have the assistance of counsel for his defense.

Amendment 7

In suits at common law, where the value in controversy shall exceed twenty dollars, the right of trial by jury shall be preserved, and no fact tried by a jury, shall be otherwise reexamined in any court of the United States, than according to the rules of the common law.

Amendment 8

Excessive bail shall not be required, nor excessive fines imposed, nor cruel and unusual punishments inflicted.

Amendment 9

The enumeration in the Constitution, of certain rights, shall not be construed to deny or disparage others retained by the people.

Amendment 10

The powers not delegated to the United States by the Constitution, nor prohibited by it to the States, are reserved to the States respectively, or to the people.

Amendments ratified December 15, 1791

1. Why do the authors of the Constitution list several rights together under the First Amendment?

2. Why do the authors say it is the right of "the people" to keep and bear arms?

3. Does the Bill of Rights tend to expand, or to limit, the range of rights a citizen can claim?

4. What do the authors mean when they state that the powers not delegated to the United States are reserved to the states *or* to the people?

5. Do the authors see law as a threat to, or as a guarantor of, rights?

6. Are the rights in the First Amendment the most important?

Declaration of the Rights of Man and the Citizen

Adopted August 26, 1789

THE REPRESENTATIVES OF THE FRENCH PEOPLE, constituted as a National Assembly, considering that ignorance, disregard or contempt of the rights of man are the sole causes of public misfortunes and governmental corruption, have resolved to set forth a solemn declaration of the natural, inalienable and sacred rights of man: in order that this declaration, by being constantly present to all members of the social body, may keep them at all times aware of their rights and duties; that the acts of both the legislative and executive powers, by being liable at every moment to comparison with the aim of all political institutions, may be the more fully respected; and that demands of the citizens, by being founded henceforward on simple and incontestable principles, may always redound to the maintenance of the constitution and the general welfare.

The Assembly consequently recognizes and declares, in the presence and under the auspices of the Supreme Being, the following rights of man and the citizen:

1. Men are born and remain free and equal in rights. Social distinctions may be based only on common utility.

2. The aim of all political association is to preserve the natural and imprescriptible rights of man. These rights are liberty, property, security and resistance to oppression.

3. The principle of all sovereignty rests essentially in the nation. No body and no individual may exercise authority which does not emanate from the nation expressly.

4. Liberty consists in the ability to do whatever does not harm another; hence the exercise of the natural rights of each man has no limits except those which assure to other members of society the enjoyment of the same rights. These limits can only be determined by law.

5. Law may rightfully prohibit only those actions which are injurious to society. No hindrance should be put in the way of anything not prohibited by law, nor may any man be forced to do what the law does not require.

6. Law is the expression of the general will. All citizens have the right to take part, in person or by their representatives, in its formation. It must be the same for all whether it protects or penalizes. All citizens being equal in its eyes are equally admissible to all public dignities, offices and employments, according to their capacity, and with no other distinction than that of their virtues and talents.

7. No man may be indicted, arrested or detained except in cases determined by law and according to the forms which it has prescribed. Those who instigate, expedite, execute or cause to be executed arbitrary orders should be punished; but any citizen summoned or seized by virtue of the law should obey instantly, and renders himself guilty by resistance.

8. Only strictly necessary punishments may be established by law, and no one may be punished except by virtue of a law established and promulgated before the time of the offense, and legally put into force.

9. Every man being presumed innocent until judged guilty, if it is deemed indispensable to keep him under arrest, all rigor not necessary to secure his person should be severely repressed by law.

10. No one may be disturbed for his opinions, even in religion, provided that their manifestation does not trouble public order as established by law.

11. Free communication of thought and opinion is one of the most precious of the rights of man. Every citizen may therefore speak, write and print freely, on his own responsibility for abuse of this liberty in cases determined by law.

12. Preservation of the rights of man and the citizen requires

the existence of public forces. These forces are therefore instituted for the advantage of all, not for the private benefit of those to whom they are entrusted.

13. For maintenance of public forces and for expenses of administration common taxation is necessary. It should be apportioned equally among all citizens according to their capacity to pay.

14. All citizens have the right, by themselves or through their representatives, to have demonstrated to them the necessity of public taxes, to consent to them freely, to follow the use made of the proceeds and to determine the shares to be paid, the means of assessment and collection and the duration.

15. Society has the right to hold accountable every public agent of administration.

16. Any society in which the guarantee of rights is not assured or the separation of powers not determined has no constitution.

17. Property being an inviolable and sacred right, no one may be deprived of it except for an obvious requirement of public necessity, certified by law, and then on condition of a just compensation in advance.

1. Why do the authors proclaim the rights of man *and* of the citizen? How, if at all, do the rights of man differ from the rights of the citizen?

2. Why does the declaration describe the rights listed as "natural, inalienable and sacred"?

3. According to the declaration, is an individual at all times obliged to obey the law?

4. Why does the declaration state that "any society in which the guarantee of rights is not assured or the separation of powers not determined has no constitution"?

5. What is meant by the declaration's claim that "men are born. . . free and equal in rights"?

6. Why does the declaration invoke the Supreme Being?

Of Civil Government
by John Locke
(selection)

Of the State of Nature

To UNDERSTAND POLITICAL POWER RIGHT, and derive it from its original, we must consider what state all men are naturally in, and that is, a state of perfect freedom to order their actions, and dispose of their possessions, and persons as they think fit, within the bounds of the law of nature, without asking leave, or depending upon the will of any other man.

A state also of equality, wherein all the power and jurisdiction is reciprocal, no one having more than another: there being nothing more evident, than that creatures of the same species and rank promiscuously born to all the same advantages of nature, and the use of the same faculties, should also be equal one amongst another without subordination or subjection, unless the lord and master of them all, should by any manifest declaration of his will set one above another, and confer on him by an evident and clear appointment an undoubted right to dominion and sovereignty. . . .

But though this be a state of liberty, yet it is not a state of licence, though man in that state have an uncontrollable liberty, to dispose of his person or possessions, yet he has not liberty to destroy himself, or so much as any creature in his possession, but where some nobler use, than its bare preservation calls for it. The state of nature has a law of nature to govern it, which obliges everyone: and reason, which is that law, teaches all mankind, who will but consult it, that being all equal and independent, no one ought to harm another in his life, health, liberty, or possessions. For men being all the workmanship of one omnipotent, and infinitely wise Maker; all the servants of one sovereign master, sent into the world by his order and about his business, they are his property, whose workmanship they are, made to last during his, not one another's pleasure. And being furnished with like faculties, sharing all in one community of nature, there cannot be supposed any such subordination among us, that may authorize us to destroy one another, as if we were made for one another's uses, as the inferior ranks of creatures are for ours. Everyone as he is bound to preserve himself, and not to quit his station wilfully; so by the like reason when his own preservation comes not in competition, ought he, as much as he can, to preserve the rest of mankind, and may not unless it be to do justice on an offender, take away, or impair the life, or what tends to the preservation of the life, the liberty, health, limb or goods of another.

And that all men may be restrained from invading others' rights, and from doing hurt to one another, and the law of nature be observed, which willeth the peace and preservation of all mankind, the execution of the law of nature is in that state, put into every man's hands, whereby everyone has a right to punish the transgressors of that law to such a degree, as may hinder its violation. For the law of nature would, as all other laws that concern men in this world, be in vain, if there were nobody that in the state of nature, had a power to execute that law, and thereby preserve the innocent and restrain offenders, and if anyone in the state of nature may punish another, for any evil he has done, everyone may do so. For in that state of perfect equality, where naturally there is no superiority or jurisdiction of one, over another, what any may do in prosecution of that law, everyone must needs have a right to do.

And thus in the state of nature, one man comes by a power

over another; but yet no absolute or arbitrary power, to use a criminal when he has got him in his hands, according to the passionate heats, or boundless extravagancy of his own will, but only to retribute to him, so far as calm reason and conscience dictates, what is proportionate to his transgression, which is so much as may serve for reparation and restraint. For these two are the only reasons, why one man may lawfully do harm to another, which is what we call punishment. In transgressing the law of nature, the offender declares himself to live by another rule, than that of reason and common equity, which is that measure God has set to the actions of men, for their mutual security: and so he becomes dangerous to mankind, the tie, which is to secure them from injury and violence, being slighted and broken by him. Which being a trespass against the whole species, and the peace and safety of it, provided for by the law of nature, every man upon this score, by the right he hath to preserve mankind in general, may restrain, or where it is necessary, destroy things noxious to them, and so may bring such evil on anyone, who hath transgressed that law, as may make him repent the doing of it, and thereby deter him, and by his example others, from doing the like mischief. . . .

Besides the crime which consists in violating the law, and varying from the right rule of reason, whereby a man so far becomes degenerate, and declares himself to quit the principles of human nature, and to be a noxious creature, there is commonly injury done to some person or other, and some other man receives damage by his transgression, in which case he who hath received any damage, has besides the right of punishment common to him with other men, a particular right to seek reparation from him that has done it. And any other person who finds it just, may also join with him that is injured, and assist him in recovering from the offender, so much as may make satisfaction for the harm he has suffered. . . .

Each transgression may be punished to that degree, and with so much severity as will suffice to make it an ill bargain to the offender, give him cause to repent, and terrify others from doing the like. Every offence that can be committed in the state of nature, may in the state of nature be also punished, equally, and as far forth as it may, in a commonwealth; for though it would be besides my present purpose, to enter here into the particulars of the law of nature, or its measures of punishment; yet, it is certain there is such a law, and that too, as intelligible and plain to a rational creature, and a studier of that law, as the positive laws of commonwealths, nay possibly plainer; as much as reason is easier to be understood, than the fancies and intricate contrivances of men. . . .

To this strange doctrine, *viz.* that in the state of nature, everyone has the executive power of the law of nature, I doubt not but it will be objected, that it is unreasonable for men to be judges in their own cases, that self-love will make men partial to themselves and their friends. And on the other side, that ill nature, passion and revenge will carry them too far in punishing others. And hence nothing but confusion and disorder will follow, and that therefore God hath certainly appointed government to restrain the partiality and violence of men [Romans 13:4]. I easily grant, that civil government is the proper remedy for the inconveniences of the state of nature, which must certainly be great, where men may be judges in their own case, since 'tis easily to be imagined, that he who was so unjust as to do his brother an injury, will scarce be so just as to condemn himself for it: but I shall desire those who make this objection, to remember that absolute monarchs are but men, and if government is to be the remedy of those evils, which necessarily follow from men's being judges in their own cases, and the state of nature is therefore not [to] be endured, I desire to know what kind of government that is, and how much better it is than the state of nature, where one man commanding a multitude, has the liberty to be judge in his own case, and may do to all his subjects whatever he pleases, without the least liberty to anyone to question or control those who execute his pleasure? And in whatsoever he doth, whether led by reason, mistake or passion, must be submitted to? Much better it is in the state of nature wherein men are not bound to submit to the unjust will of another: and if he that judges, judges amiss in his own, or any other case, he is answerable for it to the rest of mankind.

'Tis often asked as a mighty objection, where are, or ever

were, there any men in such a state of nature? To which it may suffice as an answer at present; that since all princes and rulers of independent governments all through the world, are in a state of nature, 'tis plain the world never was, nor ever will be, without numbers of men in that state. I have named all governors of independent communities, whether they are, or are not, in league with others: for 'tis not every compact that puts an end to the state of nature between men, but only this one of agreeing together mutually to enter into one community, and make one body politic; other promises and compacts, men may make one with another, and yet still be in the state of nature. The promises and bargains for truck, etc. between the two men in the desert island, . . . or between a Swiss and an Indian, in the woods of America, are binding to them, though they are perfectly in a state of nature, in reference to one another. For truth and keeping of faith belongs to men, as men, and not as members of society.

To those that say, there were never any men in the state of nature; I . . . affirm, that all men are naturally in that state, and remain so, till by their own consents they make themselves members of some politic society. . . .

Of the State of War

And here we have the plain difference between the state of nature, and the state of war, which however some men have confounded, [yet] are as far distant, as a state of peace, good will, mutual assistance, and preservation, and a state of enmity, malice, violence, and mutual destruction are one from another. Men living together according to reason, without a common superior on earth, with authority to judge between them, is properly the state of nature. But force, or a declared design of force upon the person of another, where there is no common superior on earth to appeal to for relief, is the state of war: and 'tis the want of such an appeal gives a man the right of war even against an aggressor, though he be in society and a fellow subject. Thus a thief, whom I cannot harm but by appeal to the law, for having stolen all that I am worth, I may kill, when he sets on me to rob me, but of my horse or coat: because the law, which was made for my preservation, where it cannot interpose to secure my life from present force, which if lost, is capable of no reparation, permits me my own defence, and the right of war, a liberty to kill the aggressor, because the aggressor allows not time to appeal to our common judge, nor the decision of the law, for remedy in a case, where the mischief may be irreparable. Want of a common judge with authority, puts all men in a state of nature: force without right, upon a man's person, makes a state of war, both where there is, and is not, a common judge.

But when the actual force is over, the state of war ceases between those that are in society, and are equally on both sides subjected to the fair determination of the law; because then there lies open the remedy of appeal for the past injury, and to prevent future harm. . . .

Of Slavery

The natural liberty of man is to be free from any superior power on earth, and not to be under the will or legislative authority of man, but to have only the law of nature for his rule. The liberty of man, in society, is to be under no other legislative power, but that established, by consent, in the commonwealth, nor under the dominion of any will, or restraint of any law, but what the legislative shall enact, according to the trust put in it. Freedom then is not what Sir Robert Filmer tells us, "a liberty for everyone to do what he lists, to live as he pleases, and not to be tied by any laws": but freedom of men under government, is, to have a standing rule to live by, common to everyone of that society, and made by the legislative power erected in it; a liberty to follow my own will in all things, where the rule prescribes not; and not to be subject to the inconstant, uncertain, unknown, arbitrary will of another man. As freedom of nature is to be under no other restraint but the law of nature.

This freedom from absolute, arbitrary power, is so necessary to, and closely joined with a man's preservation, that he cannot part with it, but by what forfeits his preservation and life together. . . .

Of Property

God, who hath given the world to men in common, hath also given them reason to make use of it to the best advantage of life, and convenience. The earth, and all that is therein, is given to men for the support and comfort of their being. And though all the fruits it naturally produces, and beasts it feeds, belong to mankind in common, as they are produced by the spontaneous hand of nature; and nobody has originally a private dominion, exclusive of the rest of mankind, in any of them, as they are thus in their natural state: yet being given for the use of men, there must of necessity be a means to appropriate them some way or other before they can be of any use, or at all beneficial to any particular man. . . .

Though the earth, and all inferior creatures be common to all men, yet every man has a property in his own person. This nobody has any right to but himself. The labor of his body, and the work of his hands, we may say, are properly his. Whatsoever then he removes out of the state that nature hath provided, and left it in, he hath mixed his labor with, and joined to it something that is his own, and thereby makes it his property. It being by him removed from the common state nature placed it in, it hath by this labor something annexed to it, that excludes the common right of other men. For this labor being the unquestionable property of the laborer, no man but he can have a right to what that is once joined to, at least where there is enough, and as good left in common for others.

He that is nourished by the acorns he picked up under an oak, or the apples he gathered from the trees in the wood, has certainly appropriated them to himself. Nobody can deny but the nourishment is his. I ask then, when did they begin to be his? When he digested? Or when he eat? Or when he boiled? Or when he brought them home? Or when he picked them up? And 'tis plain, if the first gathering made them not his, nothing else could. That labor put a distinction between them and common. . . .

It will perhaps be objected to this, that if gathering the acorns, or other fruits of the earth, etc. makes a right to them, then anyone may engross as much as he will. To which I answer, not so. The same law of nature, that does by this means give us property, does also bound that property too. "God has given us all things richly" (I Timothy 6:17) is the voice of reason confirmed by inspiration. But how far has he given it us? "To enjoy." As much as anyone can make use of to any advantage of life before it spoils; so much he may by his labor fix a property in. Whatever is beyond this, is more than his share, and belongs to others. Nothing was made by God for man to spoil or destroy. . . .

But the chief matter of property being now not the fruits of the earth, and the beasts that subsist on it, but the earth itself; as that which takes in and carries with it all the rest: I think it is plain, that property in that too is acquired as the former. As much land as a man tills, plants, improves, cultivates, and can use the product of, so much is his property. He by his labor does, as it were, enclose it from the common. . . .

Nor was this appropriation of any parcel of land, by improving it, any prejudice to any other man, since there was still enough, and as good left; and more than the yet unprovided could use. So that in effect, there was never the less left for others because of his enclosure for himself. For he that leaves as much as another can make use of, does as good as take nothing at all. Nobody could think himself injured by the drinking of another man, though he took a good draught, who had a whole river of the same water left him to quench his thirst. And the case of land and water, where there is enough of both, is perfectly the same. . . .

Before the appropriation of land, he who gathered as much of the wild fruit, killed, caught, or tamed, as many of the beasts as he could; he that so employed his pains about any of the spontaneous products of nature, as any way to alter them, from the state which nature put them in, by placing any of his labor on them, did thereby acquire a propriety in them: but if they perished, in his possession, without their due use; if the fruits rotted, or the venison putrefied, before he could spend it, he offended against the common law of nature, and was liable to be punished; he invaded his neighbor's share, for he had no right, further than his use called for any of them, and they might serve to afford him conveniences of life. . . .

And thus, . . . supposing the world given as it was to the children of men in common, we see how labor could make men distinct titles to several parcels of it, for their private uses; wherein there could be no doubt of right, no room for quarrel.

Nor is it so strange, as perhaps before consideration it may appear, that the property of labor should be able to overbalance the community of land. For 'tis labor indeed that puts the difference of value on everything; and let anyone consider, what the difference is between an acre of land planted with tobacco, or sugar, sown with wheat or barley; and an acre of the same land lying in common, without any husbandry upon it, and he will find, that the improvement of labor makes the far greater part of the value. . . .

Of Political or Civil Society

Man being born, as has been proved, with a title to perfect freedom, and an uncontrolled enjoyment of all the rights and privileges of the law of nature, equally with any other man, or number of men in the world, hath by nature a power, not only to preserve his property, that is, his life, liberty and estate, against the injuries and attempts of other men; but to judge of, and punish the breaches of that law in others, as he is persuaded the offence deserves, even with death itself, in crimes where the heinousness of the fact, in his opinion, requires it. But because no political society can be, nor subsist without having in itself the power to preserve the property, and in order thereunto punish the offences of all those of that society; there, and there only is political society, where every one of the members hath quitted this natural power, resigned it up into the hands of the community in all cases that exclude him not from appealing for protection to the law established by it. And thus all private judgment of every particular member being excluded, the community comes to be umpire, by settled standing rules, indifferent, and the same to all parties; and by men having authority from the community, for the execution of those rules, decides all the differences that may happen between any members of that society, concerning any matter of right; and punishes those offences, which any member hath committed against the society, with such penalties as the law has established: whereby it is easy to discern who are, and who are not, in political society together. Those who are united into one body, and have a common established law and judicature to appeal to, with authority to decide controversies between them, and punish offenders, are in civil society one with another: but those who have no such common appeal, I mean on earth, are still in the state of nature, each being, where there is no other, judge for himself, and executioner; which is, as I have before showed it, the perfect state of nature.

And thus the commonwealth comes by a power to set down, what punishment shall belong to the several transgressions which they think worthy of it, committed amongst the members of that society, (which is the power of making laws) as well as it has the power to punish any injury done unto any of its members, by anyone that is not of it, (which is the power of war and peace;) and all this for the preservation of the property of all the members of that society, as far as is possible. . . .

Of the Beginning of Political Societies

Every man being, as has been showed, naturally free, and nothing being able to put him into subjection to any earthly power, but only his own consent; it is to be considered, what shall be understood to be a sufficient declaration of a man's consent, to make him subject to the laws of any government. There is a common distinction of an express and a tacit consent, which will concern our present case. Nobody doubts but an express consent, of any man, entering into any society, makes him a perfect member of that society, a subject of that government. The difficulty is, what ought to be looked upon as a tacit consent, and how far it binds, i.e. how far anyone shall be looked on to have consented, and thereby submitted to any government, where he has made no expressions of it at all. And to this I say, that every man, that hath any possession, or enjoyment, of any part of the dominions of any government, doth thereby give his tacit consent, and is as far forth obliged to obedience to the laws of that government, during such enjoyment, as anyone under it; whether this his possession be of land, to him and his heirs for ever, or a lodging only for a week; or whether it be barely travelling freely on the highway; and in effect, it reaches as far as the very being of anyone within the territories of that government. . . .

But submitting to the laws of any country, living quietly, and enjoying privileges and protection under them, makes not a man a member of that society. . . . Nothing can make any man so, but his actually entering into it by positive engagement, and express promise and compact. This is that, which I think, concerning the beginning of political societies, and that consent which makes anyone a member of any commonwealth.

Of the Ends of Political Society and Government

If man in the state of nature be so free, as has been said; if he be absolute lord of his own person and possessions, equal to the greatest, and subject to nobody, why will he part with his freedom? Why will he give up this empire, and subject himself to the dominion and control of any other power? To which 'tis obvious to answer, that though in the state of nature he hath such a right, yet the enjoyment of it is very uncertain, and constantly exposed to the invasion of others. . . . This makes him willing to quit this condition, which however free, is full of fears and continual dangers: and 'tis not without reason, that he seeks out, and is willing to join in society with others who are already united, or have a mind to unite for the mutual preservation of their lives, liberties and estates, which I call by the general name, property.

The great and chief end therefore, of men's uniting into commonwealths, and putting themselves under government, is the preservation of their property. To which in the state of nature there are many things wanting. . . .

Thus mankind, notwithstanding all the privileges of the state of nature, being but in an ill condition, while they remain in it, are quickly driven into society. Hence it comes to pass, that we seldom find any number of men live any time together in this state. The inconveniences, that they are therein exposed to, by the irregular and uncertain exercise of the power every man has of punishing the transgressions of others, make them take sanctuary under the established laws of government, and therein seek the preservation of their property. 'Tis this make them so willingly give up everyone his single power of punishing to be exercised by such alone as shall be appointed to it amongst them; and by such rules as the community, or those authorized by them to that purpose, shall agree on. And in this we have the original right and rise of both the legislative and executive power, as well as of the governments and societies themselves.

For in the state of nature, to omit the liberty he has of innocent delights, a man has two powers.

The first is to do whatsoever he thinks fit for the preservation of himself and others within the permission of the law of nature. . . .

The other power a man has in the state of nature, is the power to punish the crimes committed against that law. Both these he gives up, when he joins in a private, if I may so call it, or particular political society, and incorporates into any commonwealth, separate from the rest of mankind.

The first power, *viz.* of doing whatsoever he thought fit for the preservation of himself, and the rest of mankind, he gives up to be regulated by laws made by the society, so far forth as the preservation of himself, and the rest of that society shall require; which laws of the society in many things confine the liberty he had by the law of nature.

Secondly, the power of punishing he wholly gives up, and engages his natural force . . . to assist the executive power of the society, as the law thereof shall require. For being now in a new state, wherein he is to enjoy many conveniences, from the labor, assistance, and society of others in the same community, as well as protection from its whole strength; he is to part also with as much of his natural liberty in providing for himself, as the good, prosperity, and safety of the society shall require: which is not only necessary, but just; since the other members of the society do the like.

But though men when they enter into society, give up the equality, liberty, and executive power they had in the state of nature, into the hands of the society, to be so far disposed of by the legislative, as the good of the society shall require; yet it being only with an intention in everyone the better to preserve himself his liberty and property; (for no rational creature can be supposed to change his condition with an intention to be worse) the power of the society, or legislative constituted by them, can never be supposed to extend further than the common good. . . . And so whoever has the legislative or supreme power of any commonwealth, is bound to govern by established standing laws, promulgated and known to the people, and not by extemporary decrees; by indifferent and upright judges, who are to decide controversies by those laws; and to employ the force of the community at home, only in the execution of such laws, or abroad to prevent or redress foreign injuries, and secure the community from inroads and invasion. And all this to be directed to no other end, but the peace, safety, and public good of the people.

—*1689*

1. Why does Locke hold that property is the reason for the establishment of civil society?

2. Why does Locke place limits on a man's liberty in the state of nature?

3. Why does Locke say that man in the state of nature has not only the right to preserve himself, but also the right "to preserve mankind in general"?

4. When an individual joins a commonwealth, does he give up any of the equality he had in the state of nature?

5. Does Locke's argument for natural right require a belief in God?

6. If the law of nature is insufficient to guarantee our lives, liberties and estates, why is Locke so careful to ground civil rights in natural right?

Anarchical Fallacies*
by Jeremy Bentham
(selection)

Preliminary Observations

IN A WORK OF SUCH EXTREME IMPORTANCE with a view to practice, and which throughout keeps practice so closely and immediately and professedly in view, a single error may be attended with the most fatal consequences. The more extensive the propositions, the more consummate will be the knowledge, the more exquisite the skill, indispensably requisite to confine them in all points within the pale of truth. The most consummate ability in the whole nation could not have been too much for the task—one may venture to say, it would not have been equal to it. But that, in the sanctioning of each proposition, the most consummate ability should happen to be vested in the heads of the sorry majority in whose hands the plenitude of power happened on that same occasion to be vested, is an event against which the chances are almost as infinity to one.

Here, then, is a radical and all-pervading error—the attempting to give to a work on such a subject the sanction of government; especially of such a government—a government com-

---

*Full title: Anarchical Fallacies; being an examination of the Declaration of Rights issued during the French Revolution

posed of members so numerous, so unequal in talent, as well as discordant in inclinations and affections. Had it been the work of a single hand, and that a private one, and in that character given to the world, every good effect would have been produced by it that could be produced by it when published as the work of government, without any of the bad effects which in case of the smallest error must result from it when given as the work of government.

The revolution, which threw the government into the hands of the penners and adopters of this declaration, having been the effect of insurrection, the grand object evidently is to justify the cause. But by justifying it, they invite it: in justifying past insurrection, they plant and cultivate a propensity to perpetual insurrection in time future; they sow the seeds of anarchy broad-cast: in justifying the demolition of existing authorities, they undermine all future ones, their own consequently in the number. Shallow and reckless vanity!—They imitate in their conduct the author of that fabled law, according to which the assassination of the prince upon the throne gave to the assassin a title to succeed him. *"People, behold your rights! If a single article of them be violated, insurrection is not your right only, but the most sacred of your duties."* Such is the constant language, for such is the professed object of this source and model of all laws—this self-consecrated oracle of all nations. . . .

Is the provision in question fit in point of expediency to be passed into a law for the government of the French nation? That, *mutatis mutandis* [with the necessary changes], would have been the question put in England: that was the proper question to have been put in relation to each provision it was proposed should enter into the composition of the body of French laws.

Instead of that, as often as the utility of a provision appeared (by reason of the wideness of its extent, for instance) of a doubtful nature, the way taken to clear the doubt was to assert it to be a provision fit to be made law for all men—for all Frenchmen—and for all Englishmen, for example, into the bargain. This medium of proof was the more alluring, inasmuch as to the advantage of removing opposition, was added the pleasure, the sort of titillation so exquisite to the nerve of vanity in a French heart—the satisfaction, to use a homely, but not the less apposite proverb, of teaching grandmothers to suck eggs. Hark! ye citizens of the other side of the water! Can you tell us what rights you have belonging to you? No, that you can't. It's *we* that understand rights: not our own only, but yours into the bargain; while you poor simple souls! know nothing about the matter.

Hasty generalization, the great stumbling block of intellectual vanity!—hasty generalization, the rock that even genius itself is so apt to split upon!—hasty generalization, the bane of prudence and of science! . . .

The great enemies of public peace are the selfish and dissocial passions:—necessary as they are—the one to the very existence of each individual, the other to his security. On the part of these affections, a deficiency in point of strength is never to be apprehended: all that is to be apprehended in respect of them, is to be apprehended on the side of their excess. Society is held together only by the sacrifices that men can be induced to make of the gratifications they demand: to obtain these sacrifices is the great difficulty, the great task of government. What has been the object, the perpetual and palpable object, of this declaration of pretended rights? To add as much force as possible to these passions, already but too strong,—to burst the cords that hold them in,—to say to the selfish passions, there—everywhere—is your prey!—to the angry passions, there—everywhere—is your enemy. . . .

The logic of it is of a piece with its morality:—a perpetual vein of nonsense, flowing from a perpetual abuse of words,—words having a variety of meanings, where words with single meanings were equally at hand—the same words used in a variety of meanings in the same page,—words used in meanings not their own, where proper words were equally at hand. . . .

In a play or a novel, an improper word is but a word: and the impropriety, whether noticed or not, is attended with no consequences. In a body of laws—especially of laws given as constitutional and fundamental ones—an improper word may be a national calamity:—and civil war may be the consequence of it. Out of one foolish word may start a thousand daggers. . . .

Article I

Men (all men) are born and remain free, and equal in respect of rights. Social distinctions cannot be founded, but upon common utility. . . .

All men born free? Absurd and miserable nonsense! When the great complaint—a complaint made perhaps by the very same people at the same time, is—that so many men are born slaves. Oh! but when we acknowledge them to be born slaves, we refer to the laws in being; which laws being void, as being contrary to those laws of nature which are the efficient causes of those rights of man that we are declaring, the men in question are free in one sense, though slaves in another;—slaves, and free, at the same time:—free in respect of the laws of nature—slaves in respect of the pretended human laws, which, though called laws, are no laws at all, as being contrary to the laws of nature. For such is the difference—the great and perpetual difference, betwixt the good subject, the rational censor of the laws, and the anarchist—between the moderate man and the man of violence. The rational censor, acknowledging the existence of the law he disapproves, proposes the repeal of it: the anarchist, setting up his will and fancy for a law before which all mankind are called upon to bow down at the first word—the anarchist, trampling on truth and decency, denies the validity of the law in question,—denies the existence of it in the character of a law, and calls upon all mankind to rise up in a mass, and resist the execution of it.

All men are born equal in rights. The rights of the heir of the most indigent family equal to the rights of the heir of the most wealthy? In what case is this true? I say nothing of hereditary *dignities* and *powers*. Inequalities such as these being proscribed under and by the French government in France, are consequently proscribed by that government under every other government, and consequently have no existence anywhere. For the total subjection of every other government to French government, is a fundamental principle in the law of universal independence—the French law. . . .

All men (i.e., all human creatures of both sexes) *remain equal in rights.* All men, meaning doubtless all human creatures. The apprentice, then, is equal in rights to his master; he has as much liberty with relation to the master, as the master has with relation to him; he has as much right to command and to punish him; he is as much owner and master of the master's house, as the master himself. The case is the same as between ward and guardian. So again as between wife and husband. The madman has as good a right to confine anybody else, as anybody else has to confine him. The idiot has as much right to govern everybody, as anybody can have to govern him. The physician and the nurse, when called in by the next friend of a sick man seized with a delirium, have no more right to prevent his throwing himself out of the window, than he has to throw them out of it. All this is plainly and incontestably included in this article of the Declaration of Rights: in the very words of it, and in the meaning—if it have any meaning. . . .

Article II

The end in view of every political association is the preservation of the natural and imprescriptible rights of man. These rights are liberty, property, security, and resistance to oppression. . . .

More confusion—more nonsense,—and the nonsense, as usual, dangerous nonsense. The words can scarcely be said to have a meaning: but if they have, or rather if they had a meaning, these would be the propositions either asserted or implied:

1. That there are such things as rights anterior to the establishment of governments: for natural, as applied to rights, if it mean anything, is meant to stand in opposition to *legal*,—to such rights as are acknowledged to owe their existence to government, and are consequently posterior in their date to the establishment of government.

2. That these rights *can not* be abrogated by government: for *can not* is implied in the form of the word imprescriptible, and the sense it wears when so applied, is the cutthroat sense above explained.

3. That the governments that exist derive their origin from formal associations, or what are now called *conventions*: associations entered into by a partnership contract, with all the members for partners,—entered into at a day prefixed, for a predetermined purpose, the formation of a new government

where there was none before (for as to formal meetings holden under the control of an existing government, they are evidently out of question here) in which it seems again to be implied in the way of inference, though a necessary and an unavoidable inference, that all governments (that is, self-called governments, knots of persons exercising the powers of government) that have had any other origin than an association of the above description, are illegal, that is, no governments at all; resistance to them, and subversion of them, lawful and commendable; and so on.

Such are the notions implied in this first part of the article. How stands the truth of things? That there are no such things as natural rights—no such things as rights anterior to the establishment of government—no such things as natural rights opposed to, in contradistinction to, legal: that the expression is merely figurative; that when used in the moment you attempt to give it a literal meaning it leads to error, and to that sort of error that leads to mischief—to the extremity of mischief.

We know what it is for men to live without government—and living without government, to live without rights: we know what it is for men to live without government, for we see instances of such a way of life—we see it in many savage nations, or rather races of mankind; for instance, among the savages of New South Wales, whose way of living is so well known to us: no habit of obedience, and thence no government—no government, and thence no laws—no laws, and thence no such things as rights—no security—no property:—liberty, as against regular control, the control of laws and government—perfect; but as against all irregular control, the mandates of stronger individuals, none. In this state, at a time earlier than the commencement of history—in this same state, judging from analogy, we, the inhabitants of the part of the globe we call Europe, were;—no government, consequently no rights: no rights, consequently no property—no legal security—no legal liberty: security not more than belongs to beasts—forecast and sense of insecurity keener—consequently in point of happiness below the level of the brutal race.

In proportion to the want of happiness resulting from the

want of rights, a reason exists for wishing that there were such things as rights. But reasons for wishing there were such things as rights, are not rights;—a reason for wishing that a certain right were established, is not that right—want is not supply—hunger is not bread.

That which has no existence cannot be destroyed—that which cannot be destroyed cannot require anything to preserve it from destruction. *Natural rights* is simple nonsense: natural and imprescriptible rights, rhetorical nonsense,—nonsense upon stilts. But this rhetorical nonsense ends in the old strain of mischievous nonsense: for immediately a list of these pretended natural rights is given, and those are so expressed as to present to view legal rights. And of these rights, whatever they are, there is not, it seems, any one of which any government *can*, upon any occasion whatever, abrogate the smallest particle.

So much for terrorist language. What is the language of reason and plain sense upon this same subject? That in proportion as it is *right* or *proper*, i.e., advantageous to the society in question, that this or that right—a right to this or that effect—should be established and maintained, in that same proportion it is *wrong* that it should be abrogated: but that as there is no *right*, which ought not to be maintained so long as it is upon the whole advantageous to the society that it should be maintained, so there is no right which, when the abolition of it is advantageous to society, should not be abolished. To know whether it would be more for the advantage of society that this or that right should be maintained or abolished, the time at which the question about maintaining or abolishing is proposed, must be given, and the circumstances under which it is proposed to maintain or abolish it; the right itself must be specifically described, not jumbled with an undistinguishable heap of others, under any such vague general terms as property, liberty, and the like.

One thing, in the midst of all this confusion, is but too plain. They know not of what they are talking under the name of natural rights and yet they would have them imprescriptible—proof against all the power of the laws—pregnant with occasions summoning the members of the community to rise up in resistance against the laws. What, then, was their object in declaring the existence of imprescriptible rights, and without specifying a single one by any such mark as it could be known by? This and no other—to excite and keep up a spirit of resistance to all laws—a spirit of insurrection against all governments—against the governments of all other nations instantly,—against the government of their own nation—against the government they themselves were pretending to establish. . . .

What is the real source of these imprescriptible rights—these unrepealable laws? Power turned blind by looking from its own height: self-conceit and tyranny exalted into insanity. No man was to have any other man for a servant, yet all men were forever to be their slaves. Making laws with imposture in their mouths, under pretence of declaring them—giving for laws anything that came uppermost, and these unrepealable ones, on pretence of finding them ready made. Made by what? Not by a God—they allow of none; but by their goddess, Nature.

The origination of governments from a contract is a pure fiction, or in other words, a falsehood. It never has been known to be true in any instance; the allegation of it does mischief, by involving the subject in error and confusion, and is neither necessary nor useful to any good purpose.

All governments that we have any account of have been gradually established by habit, after having been formed by force; unless in the instance of governments formed by individuals who have been emancipated, or have emancipated themselves, from governments already formed, the governments under which they were born—a rare case, and from which nothing follows with regard to the rest. What signifies it how governments are formed? Is it the less proper the less conducive to the happiness of society—that the happiness of society should be the one object kept in view by the members of the government in all their measures? Is it the less the interest of men to be happy—less to be wished that they may be so—less the moral duty of their governors to make them so, as far as they can, at Mogadore than at Philadelphia? . . .

Observe the extent of these pretended rights, each of them belonging to every man, and all of them without bounds. Unbounded liberty; that is, amongst other things, the liberty of doing or not doing on every occasion whatever each man pleases:—Unbounded property; that is, the right of doing with everything around him (with every *thing* at least, if not with every person,) whatsoever he pleases; communicating that right to anybody, and withholding it from anybody:—Unbounded security; that is, security for such his liberty, for such his property, and for his person, against every defalcation that can be called for on any account in respect of any of them:—Unbounded resistance to oppression; that is, unbounded exercise of the faculty of guarding himself against whatever unpleasant circumstance may present itself to his imagination or his passions under that name. . . .

Unbounded liberty—I must still say unbounded liberty;—for though the next article but one returns to the charge, and gives such a definition of liberty as seems intended to set bounds to it, yet in effect the limitation amounts to nothing; and when, as here, no warning is given of any exception in the texture of the general rule, every exception which turns up is, not a confirmation but a contradiction of the rule:—liberty, without any preannounced or intelligible bounds; and as to the other rights, they remain unbounded to the end: rights of man composed of a system of contradictions and impossibilities.

In vain would it be said, that though no bounds are here assigned to any of these rights, yet it is to be understood as taken for granted, and tacitly admitted and assumed, that they are to have bounds; *viz.* such bounds as it is understood will be set them by the laws. Vain, I say, would be this apology; for the supposition would be contradictory to the express declaration of the article itself, and would defeat the very object which the whole declaration has in view. It would be self-contradictory, because these rights are, in the same breath in which their existence is declared, declared to be imprescriptible; and imprescriptible, or, as we in England should say, indefeasible, means nothing unless it exclude the interference of the laws.

It would be not only inconsistent with itself, but inconsistent with the declared and sole object of the declaration, if it did not exclude the interference of the laws. It is against the laws themselves, and the laws only, that this declaration is levelled. It is for the hands of the legislator and all legislators, and none but legislators, that the shackles it provides are intended,—it is against the apprehended encroachments of legislators that the rights in question, the liberty and property, and so forth, are intended to be made secure,—it is to such encroachments, and damages, and dangers, that whatever security it professes to give has respect. Precious security for unbounded rights against legislators, if the extent of those rights in every direction were purposely left to depend upon the will and pleasure of those very legislators! . . .

Article IV

Liberty consists in being able to do that which is not hurtful to another, and therefore the exercise of the natural rights of each man has no other bounds than those which insure to the other members of the society the enjoyment of the same rights. These bounds cannot be determined but by the law. . . .

These bounds cannot be determined but by the law. More contradiction, more confusion. What then?—this liberty, this right, which is one of four rights that existed before laws, and will exist in spite of all that laws can do, owes all the boundaries it has, all the extent it has, to the laws. Till you know what the laws say to it, you do not know what there is of it, nor what account to give of it: and yet it existed, and that in full force and vigour, before there were any such things as laws; and so will continue to exist, and that for ever, in spite of anything which laws can do to it. Still the same inaptitude of expressions—still the same confusion of that which it is supposed *is*, with that which it is conceived ought to be.

What says plain truth upon this subject? What is the sense most approaching to this nonsense?

The liberty which the law *ought* to allow of, and leave in existence—leave uncoerced, unremoved—is the liberty which concerns those acts only, by which, if exercised, no damage would be done to the community upon the whole; that is, either no damage at all, or none but what promises to be compensated by at least equal benefit.

Accordingly, the exercise of the rights allowed to and conferred upon each individual, ought to have no other bounds set to it by the law, than those which are necessary to enable it to maintain every other individual in the possession and exercise of such rights as it is consistent with the greatest good of the community that he should be allowed. The marking out of these bounds ought not to be left to anybody but the legislator acting as such—that is, to him or them who are acknowledged to be in possession of the sovereign power: that is, it ought not to be left to the occasional and arbitrary declaration of any individual, whatever share he may possess of subordinate authority. . . .

Conclusion

What, then, shall we say of that system of government, of which the professed object is to call upon the untaught and unlettered multitude (whose existence depends upon their devoting their whole time to the acquisition of the means of supporting it,) to occupy themselves without ceasing upon all questions of government (legislation and administration included) without exception—important and trivial,—the most general and the most particular, but more especially upon the most important and most general—that is, in other words, the most scientific—those that require the greatest measures of science to qualify a man for deciding upon, and in respect of which any want of science and skill are liable to be attended with the most fatal consequences? . . .

If a collection of general propositions, put together with the design that seems to have given birth to this performance—propositions of the most general and extensive import, embracing the whole field of legislation—were capable of being so worded and put together as to be of use, it could only be on the condition of their being deduced in the way of abridgment from an already formed and existing assemblage of less general propositions, constituting the tenor of the body of the laws. But for these more general propositions to have been abstracted from that body of particular ones, that body must have been already in existence: the general and introductory part, though placed first, must have been constructed last;—although first in the order of communication, it should have been last in the order of composition. For the framing of the propositions which were to be included, time, knowledge, genius, temper, patience, everything was wanting. Yet the system of propositions which were to include them, it was determined to have at any rate. Of time, a small quantity indeed might be made to serve, upon the single and very simple condition of not bestowing a single thought upon the propositions which they were to include: and as to knowledge, genius, temper, and patience, the place of all these trivial requisites was abundantly supplied by effrontery and self-conceit. The business, instead of being performed in the way of abridgment, was performed in the way of anticipation—by a loose conjecture of what the particular propositions in question, were they to be found, might amount to.

What I mean to attack is, not the subject or citizen of this or that country—not this or that citizen—not citizen Sieyes or citizen anybody else, but all anti-legal rights of man, all declarations of such rights. What I mean to attack is, not the execution of such a design in this or that instance, but the design itself.

It is not that they have failed in their execution of the design by using the same word promiscuously in two or three senses—contradictory and incompatible senses—but in undertaking to execute a design which could not be executed at all without this abuse of words. Let a man distinguish the senses—let him allot, and allot invariably a separate word for each, and he will find it impossible to make up any such declaration at all, without running into such nonsense as must stop the hand even of the maddest of the mad.

—1796

1. Why does Bentham object so to the French Declaration of Rights?

2. Why, for Bentham, is it a "radical and all-pervading error" to give to the Declaration of Rights the sanction of government?

3. What does Bentham mean when he says that the expression "natural rights" is "merely figurative" and not literal?

4. Why does Bentham view "expediency" as the proper question to be put in relation to each provision of law?

5. Why does Bentham claim that "it's *we* [the English] that understand rights"?

6. Is Bentham correct in saying that the Declaration of Rights contains in itself "a spirit of insurrection against all governments"?

As to Humanness
by Charlotte Perkins Gilman
(selection)

PARTRIDGE-COCK, FARMYARD-COCK, peacock, from sparrow to ostrich, observe his mien! To strut and languish; to exhibit every beauteous lure; to sacrifice ease, comfort, speed, everything, to beauty—for her sake—this is the nature of the he-bird of any species; the characteristic, not of the turkey, but of the cock! With drumming of loud wings, with crow and quack and bursts of glorious song, he woos his mate; displays his splendors before her; fights fiercely with his rivals. To butt—to strut—to make a noise—all for love's sake; these acts are common to the male.

We may now generalize and clearly state: That is masculine which belongs to the male—to any or all males, irrespective of species. That is feminine which belongs to the female, to any or all females, irrespective of species. That is ovine, bovine, feline, canine, equine, or asinine which belongs to that species, irrespective of sex.

In our own species all this is changed. We have been so taken up with the phenomena of masculinity and femininity that our common humanity has largely escaped notice. We know we are human, naturally, and are very proud of it; but we do not consider in what our humanness consists, nor how men and women may fall short of it, or overstep its bounds, in continual insistence upon their special differences. It is "manly" to do this; it is "womanly" to do that; but what a human being should do

This mental attitude toward women is even more clearly expressed by Mr. H. B. Marriott-Watson in his article on "The American Woman" in the *Nineteenth Century* for June 1904, where he says: "Her constitutional restlessness has caused her to abdicate those functions which alone excuse or explain her existence." This is a peculiarly unhappy and condensed expression of the relative position of women during our androcentric culture. The man was accepted as the race type without one dissentient voice; and the woman—a strange, diverse creature, quite disharmonious in the accepted scheme of things—was excused and explained only as a female.

She has needed volumes of such excuse and explanation; also, apparently, volumes of abuse and condemnation. In any library catalogue we may find books upon books about women: physiological, sentimental, didactic, religious—all manner of books about women, as such. Even today in the works of Marholm, poor young Weininger, Mœbius, and others, we find the same perpetual discussion of women—as such. . . .

We can see at once, glaringly, what would have been the result of giving all human affairs into female hands. Such an extraordinary and deplorable situation would have "feminized" the world. We should have all become "effeminate."

See how in our use of language the case is clearly shown. The adjectives and derivatives based on woman's distinctions are alien and derogatory when applied to human affairs; "effeminate"—too female, connotes contempt, but has no masculine analogue; whereas "emasculate"—not enough male, is a term of reproach, and has no feminine analogue. "Virile"—manly, we oppose to "puerile"—childish, and the very word "virtue" is derived from "vir"—a man.

Even in the naming of other animals we have taken the male as the race type, and put on a special termination to indicate "his female," as in lion, lioness; leopard, leopardess; while all our human scheme of things rests on the same tacit assumption; man being held the human type, woman a sort of accompaniment and subordinate assistant, merely essential to the making of people.

She has held always the place of a preposition in relation to man. She has been considered above him or below him, before him, behind him, beside him, a wholly relative existence—"Sydney's sister," "Pembroke's mother"—but never by any chance Sydney or Pembroke herself.

Acting on this assumption, all human standards have been based on male characteristics, and when we wish to praise the work of a woman, we say she has "a masculine mind."

It is no easy matter to deny or reverse a universal assumption. The human mind has had a good many jolts since it began to think, but after each upheaval it settles down as peacefully as the vine-growers on Vesuvius, accepting the last lava crust as permanent ground.

What we see immediately around us, what we are born into and grow up with, be it mental furniture or physical, we assume to be the order of nature.

If a given idea has been held in the human mind for many generations, as almost all our common ideas have, it takes sincere and continued effort to remove it; and if it is one of the oldest we have in stock, one of the big, common, unquestioned world ideas, vast is the labor of those that seek to change it.

Nevertheless, if the matter is one of importance, if the previous idea was a palpable error, of large and evil effect, and if the new one is true and widely important, the effort is worth making.

The task here undertaken is of this sort. It seeks to show that what we have all this time called "human nature" and deprecated, was in great part only male nature, and good enough in its place: that what we have called "masculine" and admired as such, was in large part human, and should be applied to both sexes; that what we have called "feminine" and condemned, was also largely human and applicable to both. Our androcentric culture is so shown to have been, and still to be, a masculine culture in excess, and therefore undesirable.

In the preliminary work of approaching these facts it will be well to explain how it can be that so wide and serious an error should have been made by practically all men. The reason is simply that they were men. They were males, and saw women as females—and not otherwise.

So absolute is this conviction that the man who reads will

say, "Of course! How else are we to look at women except as females? They are females, aren't they?" Yes, they are, as men are males unquestionably; but there is possible the frame of mind of the old marquise who was asked by an English friend how she could bear to have the footman serve her breakfast in bed—to have a man in her bedchamber—and replied sincerely, "Call you that thing there a man?"

The world is full of men, but their principal occupation is human work of some sort; and women see in them the human distinction preponderantly. Occasionally some unhappy lady marries her coachman—long contemplation of broad shoulders having an effect, apparently; but in general women see the human creature most, the male creature only when they love.

To the man, the whole world was his world, his because he was male; and the whole world of woman was the home, because she was female. She had her prescribed sphere, strictly limited to her feminine occupations and interests; he had all the rest of life, and not only so, but, having it, insisted on calling it male.

This accounts for the general attitude of men toward the now rapid humanization of women. From her first faint struggles toward freedom and justice, to her present valiant efforts toward full economic and political equality, each step has been termed "unfeminine," and resented as an intrusion upon man's place and power. Here shows the need of our new classification, of the three distinct fields of life—masculine, feminine, and human.

As a matter of fact, there is a "woman's sphere," sharply defined and quite different from his; there is also a "man's sphere," as sharply defined and even more limited; but there remains a common sphere—that of humanity which belongs to both alike.

In the early part of what is known as "the woman's movement," it was sharply opposed on the ground that women would become "unsexed." Let us note in passing that they have become unsexed in one particular, most glaringly so, and no one has noticed or objected to it.

As part of our androcentric culture, we may point to the peculiar reversal of sex characteristics which makes the human female carry the burden of ornament. She alone, of all female creatures, has adopted the essentially masculine attribute of special sex-decoration; she does not fight for her mate, as yet, but she blooms forth as do the peacock and the bird of paradise, in poignant reversal of nature's laws, even wearing masculine feathers to further her feminine ends.

Woman's natural work as a female is that of the mother; man's natural work as a male is that of the father; their mutual relation to this end being a source of joy and well-being when rightly held: but human work covers all our life outside of these specialties. Every handicraft, every profession, every science, every art, all normal amusements and recreations, all government, education, religion, the whole living world of human achievement—all this is human.

That one sex should have monopolized all human activities, called them "man's work," and managed them as such, is what is meant by the phrase "androcentric culture."

—1904

1. Why does Gilman conclude that our humanness "lies in what we do and how we do it, rather than in what we are"?

2. Why does Gilman root our humanness and "even our individuality" in our social relations?

3. Why does Gilman define "human work" as separate from the "natural work" of males and females?

4. Why does Gilman say that "man's sphere" is more limited than "woman's sphere"?

5. Why does Gilman say that the only time we recognize our "common humanity" is in matters of life and death?

6. Why has no one "noticed or objected to . . . the peculiar reversal of sex characteristics which makes the human female carry the burden of ornament"?

The Four Freedoms*

(selection)

The four freedoms of common humanity are as much elements of man's needs as air and sunlight, bread and salt. Deprive him of all these freedoms and he dies—deprive him of a part of them and a part of him withers. Give them to him in full and abundant measure and he will cross the threshold of a new age, the greatest age of man.

These freedoms are the rights of men of every creed and every race, wherever they live. This is their heritage, long withheld. We of the United Nations have the power and the men and the will at last to assure man's heritage.

The belief in the four freedoms of common humanity—the belief in man, created free, in the image of God—is the crucial difference between ourselves and the enemies we face today. In it lies the absolute unity of our alliance, opposed to the oneness of the evil we hate. Here is our strength, the source and promise of victory.

— Franklin D. Roosevelt

B EYOND THE WAR LIES THE PEACE. Both sides have sketched the outlines of the new world toward which they strain. The leaders of the Axis countries have published their design for all to read. They promise a world in which the conquered

---

*From a booklet published by the Office of War Information, Washington, D.C., 1942.

peoples will live out their lives in the service of their masters.

The United Nations, now engaged in a common cause, have also published their design, and have committed certain common aims to writing. They plan a world in which men stand straight and walk free, free not of all human trouble but free of the fear of despotic power, free to develop as individuals, free to conduct and shape their affairs. Such a world has been more dream than reality, more hope than fact; but it has been the best hope men have had and the one for which they have most consistently shown themselves willing to die.

This freeness, this liberty, this precious thing men love and mean to save, is the good granite ledge on which the United Nations now propose to raise their new world after victory. The purpose of this pamphlet is to examine and define the essential freedoms.

To talk of war aims, shouting over the din of battle while the planet rocks and vibrates, may seem futile to some. Yet the talk must go on among free peoples. The faith people have in themselves is what the free have to build upon. Such faith is basic to them—man's hot belief in man, a belief which suggests that human beings are capable of ordering their affairs. This is a high compliment paid by man to himself, an evidence or gesture of self-respect, of stature, of dignity, and of worth, an affidavit of individual responsibility.

The freedoms we are fighting for, we who are free: the freedoms for which the men and women in the concentration camps and prisons and in the dark streets of the subjugated countries wait, are four in number.

"The first is freedom of speech and expression—everywhere in the world.

"The second is freedom of every person to worship God in his own way—everywhere in the world.

"The third is freedom from want—which, translated into world terms, means economic understandings which will secure to every nation a healthy peacetime life for its inhabitants—everywhere in the world.

"The fourth is freedom from fear—which, translated into world terms, means a world-wide reduction of armaments to such a point and in such a thorough fashion that no nation will be in a position to commit an act of physical aggression against any neighbor—anywhere in the world." [Franklin D. Roosevelt, January 6, 1941]

These freedoms are separate, but not independent. Each one relies upon all the others. Each supports the whole, which is liberty. When one is missing, all the others are jeopardized. A person who lives under a tyrant, and has lost freedom of speech, must necessarily be tortured by fear. A person who is in great want is usually also in great fear—fear of even direr want and greater insecurity. A person denied the right to worship in his own way has thereby lost the knack of free speech, for unless he is free to exercise his religious conscience, his privilege of free speech (even though not specifically denied) is meaningless. A person tortured with fears has lost both the privilege of free speech and the strength to supply himself with his needs. Clearly these four freedoms are as closely related, as dependent one upon another, as the four seasons of the natural year, whose winter snows irrigate the spring, and whose dead leaves, fermenting, rebuild the soil for summer's yield.

The first two freedoms—freedom of speech and freedom of religion—are cultural. They are prerogatives of the thinking man, of the creative and civilized human being. Sometimes, as in the United States, they are guaranteed by organic law. They are rather clearly understood, and the laws protecting them are continually being revised and adjusted to preserve their basic meaning. Freedom from fear and from want, on the other hand, are not part of our culture but part of our environment—they concern the facts of our lives rather than the thoughts of our minds. Men are unafraid, or well-fed, or both, according to the conditions under which they live.

To be free a man must live in a society which has relieved those curious pressures which conspire to make men slaves: pressure of a despotic government, pressure of intolerance, pressure of want. The declaration of the four freedoms, therefore, is not a promise of a gift which, under certain conditions, the people will receive; it is a declaration of a design which the people themselves may execute.

Freedom, of whatever sort, is relative. Nations united by a common effort to create a better world are obviously not projecting a Utopia in which nobody shall want for anything. That is not the point—nor within the range of human possibility. What unites them is the purpose to create a world in which no one need want for the minimum necessities of an orderly and decent life, for cleanliness, for self-respect and security. It is an ambitious design, perhaps too ambitious for the cynic or the faithless; but it is supported by the sure knowledge that the earth produces abundantly and that men are already in possession of the tools which could realize such a purpose if men chose to use them.

This, then, is a credo to which the representatives of 28 nations have subscribed—not a promise made by any group of men to any other group. It is only the people themselves who can create the conditions favoring these essential freedoms which they are now repurchasing in the bazaar of war and paying for with their lives. Nothing is for sale at bargain prices, nor will the house be built in three days with cheap labor. From a world in ruins there can rise only a slow, deliberate monument. This time, conceived by so many peoples of united purpose, it will rise straight upward and rest on good support.

Freedom of Speech

To live free a man must speak openly: gag him and he becomes either servile or full of cankers. Free government is then the most realistic kind of government for it not only assumes that a man has something on his mind, but concedes his right to say it. It permits him to talk—not without fear of contradiction, but without fear of punishment.

There can be no people's rule unless there is talk. Men, it turns out, breathe through their minds as well as through their lungs, and there must be a circulation of ideas as well as of air. Since nothing is likely to be more distasteful to a man than the opinion of someone who disagrees with him, it does the race credit that it has so stubbornly defended the principle of free speech. But if a man knows anything at all, he knows that that principle is fundamental in self-government, the whole purpose of which is to reflect and affirm the will of the people.

In America, free speech and a free press were the first things the minds of the people turned to after the fashioning of the Constitution. Farsighted men, in those early days, readily understood that some sort of protection was necessary. Thus when the first amendment to the Constitution was drawn (part of what the world now knows as the Bill of Rights), it prohibited the Congress from making any law which might abridge the freedom of speech or of the press, or the right of the people peaceably to assemble and to petition the Government for a redress of their grievances.

In the Nazi state, freedom of speech and expression have been discarded—not for temporary military expediency, but as a principle of life. Being contemptuous of the individual, and secretly suspicious of him, the German leader has deprived him of his voice. Ideas are what tyrants most fear. To set up a despotic state, the first step is to get rid of the talkers—the talkers in schools, the talkers in forums, the talkers in political rallies and in trade union meetings, the talkers on the radio and in the newsreels, and in the barber shops and village garages. Talk does not fit the Nazi and the Fascist scheme, where all ideas are, by the very nature of the political structure, the property of one man.

Talk is death to tyranny, for it can easily clarify a political position which the ruler may prefer to becloud, and it can expose injustices which he may choose to obscure.

Our Bill of Rights specifically mentioned the press. Today the press is one of many forms of utterance. Talk and ideas flow in ever-increasing torrents, through books, magazines, schools, the radio, the motion picture. The camera has created a whole new language of its own. . . .

The right to speak, the right to hear, the right of access to information carry with them certain responsibilities. Certain favorable conditions are necessary before freedom of speech acquires validity.

The first condition is that the individual have something to say. Literacy is a prerequisite of free speech, and gives it point. Denied education, denied information, suppressed or enslaved, people grow sluggish; their opinions are hardly worth the high privilege of release. Similarly, those who live in terror or in destitution, even though no specific control is placed upon their speech, are as good as gagged.

Another condition necessary for free speech is that the people have access to the means of uttering it—to newspapers, to the radio, the public forum. When power or capital are concentrated, when the press is too closely the property of narrow interests, then freedom suffers. There is no freedom, either, unless facts are within reach, unless information is made available. And a final condition of free speech is that there be no penalties attached to the spread of information and to the expression of opinion, whether those penalties be applied by the Government or by any private interests whatsoever.

The operation of a free press and the free expression of opinion are far from absolute rights. The laws of libel and slander set limits on what men may say of other men. The exigency of war sets limits on what information may be given out, lest it give aid and comfort to the enemy. Good taste sets limits on all speech.

Freedom of speech, Justice Holmes has warned, does not grant the right to shout fire in a crowded theatre. When ideas become overt acts against peace and order, then the Government presumes to interfere with free speech. The burden of proof, however, is upon those who would restrict speech—the danger must be not some vague danger but real and immediate.

We are not so much concerned with these inevitable limitations to free speech as with the delight at the principle in society and how greatly it has strengthened man's spirit, how steadily it has enlarged his culture and his world. We in America know what the privilege is because we have lived with it for a century and a half. Talk founded the Union, nurtured it, and preserved it. The dissenter, the disbeliever, the crack-pot, the reformer, those who would pull down as well as build up—all are free to have their say. . . .

The United States fights to preserve this heritage, which is the very essence of the Four Freedoms. How, unless there is freedom of speech, can freedom of religion or freedom from want or freedom from fear be realized? . . .

Freedom of Religion

That part of man which is called the spirit and which belongs only to himself and to his God, is of the very first concern in designing a free world. It was not their stomachs but their immortal souls which brought the first settlers to America's shores, and they prayed before they ate. Freedom of conscience, the right to worship God, is part of our soil and of the sky above this continent.

Freedom of worship implies that the individual has a source of moral values which transcends the immediate necessities of the community, however important these may be. It is one thing to pay taxes to the state—this men will do; it is another to submit their consciences to the state—this they politely decline. The wise community respects this mysterious quality in the individual, and makes its plans accordingly.

The democratic guarantee of freedom of worship is not in the nature of a grant—it is in the nature of an admission. It is the state admitting that the spirit soars in illimitable regions beyond the collectors of customs. It was Tom Paine, one of the great voices of freedom in early America, who pointed out that a government could no more grant to man the liberty to worship God than it could grant to God the liberty of receiving such worship.

The miracle which democracy has achieved is that while practicing many kinds of worship, we nevertheless achieve social unity and peace. And so we have the impressive spectacle, which is with us always here in America, of men attending many different churches, but the same town meeting, the same political forum. . . .

Freedom from Want

The proposal that want be abolished from this world would be pretentious, or even ridiculous, were it not for two important recent discoveries.

One is the discovery that, beyond any doubt, men now possess the technical ability to produce in great abundance the necessities of daily life—enough for everyone. This is a revolutionary and quite unprecedented condition on earth, which stimulates the imagination and quickens the blood.

Another is the discovery (or rather the realization) that the earth is one planet indivisible—that one man's hunger is every other man's hunger. We know now that the world must be looked at whole if men are to enjoy the fruits they are now able to produce, and if the inhabitants of the globe are to survive and prosper.

Freedom from want, everywhere in the world, is within the grasp of men. It has never been quite within their grasp before. Prosperous times have been enjoyed in certain regions of the world at certain periods in history, but local prosperity was usually achieved at the expense of some other region, which was being impoverished, and the spectre of impending war hung over all. Now, the industrial changes of the last 150 years and the new prospect implicit in the words "United Nations" have given meaning to the phrase "freedom from want" and rendered it not only possible but necessary.

It was in the year 1492 that the earth became round in the minds of men—although it had been privately globular for many centuries. Now in the year *1942*, by a coincidence which should fortify astrologers, the earth's rotundity again opens new vistas, this time not of fabulous continents ready to be ransacked, but of a fabulous world ready to be unified and restored. War having achieved totality, against men's wishes but with their full participation, our great resolve as we go to battle must now be that the peace shall be total also. The world is all one today. No military gesture anywhere on earth, however trivial, has been without consequence everywhere; and what is true of the military is true, also, of the economic. A hungry man in Cambodia is a threat to the well-fed of Duluth. . . .

Once, the soil was regarded as something to use and get the most from and then abandon. Now it is something to conserve and replenish. Once it was enough that a man compete freely in business, for the greatest possible personal gain; now his enterprise, still free, must meet social standards and must not tend toward concentration of power unfavorable to the general well-being of the community. Once, an idle man was presumed to be a loafer; now it is realized he may be a victim of circumstances in which all share, and for which all are responsible.

The great civilizations of the past were never free from widespread poverty. Very few of them, and these only during short periods, produced enough wealth to make possible a decent living standard for all their members, even if that wealth had been equally divided. In the short space of a few decades we have changed scarcity to abundance and are now engaged in the experiment of trying to live with our new and as yet unmanageable riches. The problem becomes one not of production but of distribution and of consumption; and since buying power must be earned, freedom from want becomes freedom from mass unemployment, plus freedom from penury for those individuals unable to work.

In our United States the Federal Government, being the common meeting ground of all interests and the final agency of the people, assumes a certain responsibility for the solution of economic problems. This is not a new role for the Government, which has been engaged since the earliest days of our history in devising laws and machinery and techniques for promoting the well-being of the citizen, whether he was a soldier returning from a war, or a new settler heading west to seek his fortune, or a manufacturer looking for a market for his goods, or a farmer puzzled over a problem in animal husbandry.

The beginning has been made. The right to work. The right to fair pay. The right to adequate food, clothing, shelter, medical care. The right to security. The right to live in an atmosphere of free enterprise. We state these things as "rights"—not because man has any natural right to be nourished and sheltered, not because the world owes any man a living, but because unless man succeeds in filling these primary needs his only development is backward and downward, his only growth malignant, and his last resource war.

All of these opportunities are not in the American record yet, and they are not yet in the world's portfolio in the shape of blueprints. Much of America and most of the world are not properly fed, clothed, housed. But there has never been a time, since the world began, when the hope of providing the essentials of life to every living man and woman and child has been so good, or when the necessity has been so great. . . .

Freedom from Fear

Fear is the inheritance of every animal, and man is no exception. Our children fear the tangible dark, and we give them what reassurance we can, so that they will grow and develop normally, their minds free from imaginary terrors. This reassurance, this sense of protection and security, is an important factor in their lives.

The new dark which has settled on the earth with the coming of might and force and evil has terrified grown men and women. They fear the dark, fear fire and the sword; they are tormented by the dread of evils which are only too real. They fear the conqueror who places his shackles on the mind. Above all else they are tortured by that basic political fear: fear of domination of themselves by others—others who are stronger, others who are advancing, others who have the weapons and are destroying and burning and pillaging. This is the fear which haunts millions of men and women everywhere in the world. It is the fear of being awakened in the night, with the rapping on the door.

No structure of peace, no design for a good world, will have any solidity or strength or even any meaning unless it disperses the shadow of this fear and brings reassurance to men and women, not only for themselves but for their children and their children's children. Aggressive war, sudden armed attack, secret police, these must be forever circumvented. The use of force, historically the means of settling disputes, must be made less and less feasible on earth, until it finally becomes impossible. Even though the underlying causes which foment wars may not be immediately eradicated from the earth, the physical act of war can be prevented when people, by their ingenuity, their intelligence, their memory, and their moral nature, choose to do so. Force can be eliminated as a means of political action only if it be opposed with an equal or greater force— which is economic and moral and which is backed by collective police power, so that in a community of nations no one nation or group of nations will have the opportunity to commit acts of aggression against any neighbor, anywhere in the world.

The machinery for enforcing peace is important and indispensable; but even more important is that there be established a moral situation, which will support and operate this machinery. As the last war ended, an attempt was made to construct an orderly world society capable of self-control. It was an idealistic and revolutionary plan. But like the first automobile, it moved haltingly and was more of a novelty than a success. For a while men's hopes focused on the plan; but it was never universally accepted. The faith was not there, nor the courage.

Today many nations are working together with unbelievable energy and with harmony of feeling and interest. They are united at the moment by the desire to win battles, but they are also united by common principles and by a conviction that their people ultimately want the same thing from life—freedom, peace, security, the chance to live as individuals.

Such collaboration has its origin in the democratic spirit, which infects men regardless of latitude or longitude. . . .

Freedom of speech and religion, freedom from want and from fear—these belong to all the earth and to all men everywhere. Our own country, with its ideas of equality, is an experiment which has been conducted against odds and with much patience and, best of all, with some success for most people. It has prospered and brought fresh hope to millions and new good to humanity. Even in the thick of war the experiment goes ahead with old values and new forms. Life is change. The earth shrinks in upon itself and we adjust to a world in motion, holding fast to the truth as we know it, confident that as long as the love of freedom shows in the eyes of men, it will show also in their deeds.

1. Why do the authors make a distinction between "cultural" and "environmental" freedoms? Why do they say that freedom of speech and freedom of religion are "prerogatives of the thinking man, of the creative and civilized human being"?

2. Why do the authors say that the declaration of the four freedoms is "not a promise of a gift"?

3. Why do the authors say that free government is the "most realistic kind of government"?

4. Do the authors present the discovery that "the earth is one planet indivisible" as a political reality or as a source of moral obligation?

5. Why do the authors deny that man has any "natural right to be nourished and sheltered"?

6. Why do the authors point out that the hope for a world of freedom has been "the best hope men have had and the one for which they have most consistently shown themselves willing to die"?

The Perplexities
of the Rights of Man
by Hannah Arendt

(selection)

O UT OF THE LIQUIDATION of the two multinational states of
prewar Europe, Russia and Austria-Hungary, two victim
groups emerged whose sufferings were different from those of
all others in the era between the wars; they were worse off than
the dispossessed middle classes, the unemployed, the small
rentiers, the pensioners whom events had deprived of social status, the possibility to work, and the right to hold property: they
had lost those rights which had been thought of and even defined as inalienable, namely the Rights of Man. The stateless
and the minorities, rightly termed "cousins-germane," had no
governments to represent and to protect them and therefore
were forced to live either under the law of exception of the
Minority Treaties, which all governments (except Czechoslovakia) had signed under protest and never recognized as law, or
under conditions of absolute lawlessness. . . .

The Declaration of the Rights of Man at the end of the eighteenth century was a turning point in history. It meant nothing more nor less than that from then on Man, and not God's command or the customs of history, should be the source of Law. Independent of the privileges which history had bestowed upon certain strata of society or certain nations, the declaration indicated man's emancipation from all tutelage and announced that he had now come of age. . . .

Since the Rights of Man were proclaimed to be "inalienable," irreducible to and undeducible from other rights or laws, no authority was invoked for their establishment; Man himself was their source as well as their ultimate goal. No special law, moreover, was deemed necessary to protect them because all laws were supposed to rest upon them. Man appeared as the only sovereign in matters of law as the people was proclaimed the only sovereign in matters of government. The people's sovereignty (different from that of the prince) was not proclaimed by the grace of God but in the name of Man, so that it seemed only natural that the "inalienable" rights of man would find their guarantee and become an inalienable part of the right of the people to sovereign self-government.

In other words, man had hardly appeared as a completely emancipated, completely isolated being who carried his dignity within himself without reference to some larger encompassing order, when he disappeared again into a member of a people. From the beginning the paradox involved in the declaration of inalienable human rights was that it reckoned with an "abstract" human being who seemed to exist nowhere, for even savages lived in some kind of a social order. If a tribal or other "backward" community did not enjoy human rights, it was obviously because as a whole it had not yet reached that stage of civilization, the stage of popular and national sovereignty, but was oppressed by foreign or native despots. The whole question of human rights, therefore, was quickly and inextricably blended with the question of national emancipation; only the emancipated sovereignty of the people, of one's own people, seemed to be able to insure them. As mankind, since the

French Revolution, was conceived in the image of a family of nations, it gradually became self-evident that the people, and not the individual, was the image of man.

The full implication of this identification of the rights of man with the rights of peoples in the European nation-state system came to light only when a growing number of people and peoples suddenly appeared whose elementary rights were as little safeguarded by the ordinary functioning of nation-states in the middle of Europe as they would have been in the heart of Africa. The Rights of Man, after all, had been defined as "inalienable" because they were supposed to be independent of all governments; but it turned out that the moment human beings lacked their own government and had to fall back upon their minimum rights, no authority was left to protect them and no institution was willing to guarantee them. . . .

The stateless people were as convinced as the minorities that loss of national rights was identical with loss of human rights, that the former inevitably entailed the latter. The more they were excluded from right in any form, the more they tended to look for a reintegration into a national, into their own national community. . . .

The failure of all responsible persons to meet the calamity of an ever-growing body of people forced to live outside the scope of all tangible law with the proclamation of a new bill of rights was certainly not due to ill will. Never before had the Rights of Man, solemnly proclaimed by the French and the American revolutions as the new fundament for civilized societies, been a practical political issue. During the nineteenth century, these rights had been invoked in a rather perfunctory way, to defend individuals against the increasing power of the state and to mitigate the new social insecurity caused by the industrial revolution. Then the meaning of human rights acquired a new connotation: they became the standard slogan of the protectors of the underprivileged, a kind of additional law, a right of exception necessary for those who had nothing better to fall back upon.

The reason why the concept of human rights was treated as a sort of stepchild by nineteenth-century political thought and why no liberal or radical party in the twentieth century, even when an urgent need for enforcement of human rights arose, saw fit to include them in its program seems obvious: civil rights—that is the varying rights of citizens in different countries—were supposed to embody and spell out in the form of tangible laws the eternal Rights of Man, which by themselves were supposed to be independent of citizenship and nationality. All human beings were citizens of some kind of political community; if the laws of their country did not live up to the demands of the Rights of Man, they were expected to change them, by legislation in democratic countries or through revolutionary action in despotisms.

The Rights of Man, supposedly inalienable, proved to be unenforceable—even in countries whose constitutions were based upon them—whenever people appeared who were no longer citizens of any sovereign state. To this fact, disturbing enough in itself, one must add the confusion created by the many recent attempts to frame a new bill of human rights, which have demonstrated that no one seems able to define with any assurance what these general human rights, as distinguished from the rights of citizens, really are. Although everyone seems to agree that the plight of these people consists precisely in their loss of the Rights of Man, no one seems to know which rights they lost when they lost these human rights.

The first loss which the rightless suffered was the loss of their homes, and this meant the loss of the entire social texture into which they were born and in which they established for themselves a distinct place in the world. This calamity is far from unprecedented; in the long memory of history, forced migrations of individuals or whole groups of people for political or economic reasons look like everyday occurrences. What is unprecedented is not the loss of a home but the impossibility of finding a new one. Suddenly, there was no place on earth where migrants could go without the severest restrictions, no country where they would be assimilated, no territory where they could found a new community of their own. This, moreover, had next to nothing to do with any material problem of overpopulation; it was a problem not of space but of political organization. Nobody had been aware that mankind, for so long a time considered under the image of a family of nations, had reached the stage where whoever was thrown out of one of these tightly organized closed communities found himself thrown out of the family of nations altogether.

The second loss which the rightless suffered was the loss of government protection, and this did not imply just the loss of legal status in their own, but in all countries. Treaties of reciprocity and international agreements have woven a web around the earth that makes it possible for the citizen of every country to take his legal status with him no matter where he goes. . . . Yet, whoever is no longer caught in it finds himself out of legality altogether. . . .

One of the surprising aspects of our experience with stateless people who benefit legally from committing a crime has been the fact that it seems to be easier to deprive a completely innocent person of legality than someone who has committed an offense. Anatole France's famous quip, "If I am accused of stealing the towers of Notre Dame, I can only flee the country," has assumed a horrible reality. Jurists are so used to thinking of law in terms of punishment, which indeed always deprives us of certain rights, that they may find it even more difficult than the layman to recognize that the deprivation of legality, i.e., of *all* rights, no longer has a connection with specific crimes.

This situation illustrates the many perplexities inherent in the concept of human rights. No matter how they have once been defined (life, liberty, and the pursuit of happiness, according to the American formula, or as equality before the law, liberty, protection of property, and national sovereignty, according to the French); no matter how one may attempt to improve an ambiguous formulation like the pursuit of happiness, or an antiquated one like unqualified right to property; the real situation of those whom the twentieth century has driven outside the pale of the law shows that these are rights of citizens whose loss does not entail absolute rightlessness. The soldier during the war is deprived of his right to life, the criminal of his right to freedom, all citizens during an emergency of their right to the pursuit of happiness, but nobody would ever claim that in any of these instances a loss of human rights has taken place. . . .

The calamity of the rightless is not that they are deprived of life, liberty, and the pursuit of happiness, or of equality before the law and freedom of opinion—formulas which were designed to solve problems *within* given communities—but that they no longer belong to any community whatsoever. Their plight is not that they are not equal before the law, but that no law exists for them; not that they are oppressed but that nobody wants even to oppress them. Only in the last stage of a rather lengthy process is their right to live threatened; only if they remain perfectly "superfluous," if nobody can be found to "claim" them, may their lives be in danger. Even the Nazis started their extermination of Jews by first depriving them of all legal status (the status of second-class citizenship) and cutting them off from the world of the living by herding them into ghettos and concentration camps; and before they set the gas chambers into motion they had carefully tested the ground and found out to their satisfaction that no country would claim these people. The point is that a condition of complete rightlessness was created before the right to live was challenged.

The same is true even to an ironical extent with regard to the right of freedom which is sometimes considered to be the very essence of human rights. There is no question that those outside the pale of the law may have more freedom of movement than a lawfully imprisoned criminal or that they enjoy more freedom of opinion in the internment camps of democratic countries than they would in any ordinary despotism, not to mention in a totalitarian country. But neither physical safety—being fed by some state or private welfare agency—nor freedom of opinion changes in the least their fundamental situation of rightlessness. The prolongation of their lives is due to charity and not to right, for no law exists which could force the nations to feed them; their freedom of movement, if they have it at all, gives them no right to residence which even the jailed criminal enjoys as a matter of course; and their freedom of opinion is a fool's freedom, for nothing they think matters anyhow.

These last points are crucial. The fundamental deprivation of human rights is manifested first and above all in the deprivation of a place in the world which makes opinions significant and actions effective. Something much more fundamental than freedom and justice, which are rights of citizens, is at stake when belonging to the community into which one is born is no longer a matter of course and not belonging no longer a matter of choice, or when one is placed in a situation where, unless he commits a crime, his treatment by others does not depend on what he does or does not do. This extremity, and nothing else, is the situation of people deprived of human rights. They are deprived, not of the right to freedom, but of the right to action; not of the right to think whatever they please, but of the right to opinion. Privileges in some cases, injustices in most, blessings and doom are meted out to them according to accident and without any relation whatsoever to what they do, did, or may do.

We became aware of the existence of a right to have rights (and that means to live in a framework where one is judged by one's actions and opinions) and a right to belong to some kind of organized community, only when millions of people emerged who had lost and could not regain these rights because of the new global political situation. The trouble is that this calamity arose not from any lack of civilization, backwardness, or mere tyranny, but, on the contrary, that it could not be repaired, because there was no longer any "uncivilized" spot on earth, because whether we like it or not we have really started to live in One World. Only with a completely organized humanity could the loss of home and political status become identical with expulsion from humanity altogether.

Before this, what we must call a "human right" today would have been thought of as a general characteristic of the human condition which no tyrant could take away. Its loss entails the loss of the relevance of speech (and man, since Aristotle, has been defined as a being commanding the power of speech and thought), and the loss of all human relationship (and man, again since Aristotle, has been thought of as the "political animal," that is, one who by definition lives in a community), the loss, in other words, of some of the most essential characteristics of human life. This was to a certain extent the plight of slaves, whom Aristotle therefore did not count among human beings. . . .Not the loss of specific rights, then, but the loss of a community willing and able to guarantee any rights whatsoever, has been the calamity which has befallen ever-increasing numbers of people. Man, it turns out, can lose all so-called Rights of Man without losing his essential quality as man, his human dignity. Only the loss of a polity itself expels him from humanity.

The right that corresponds to this loss and that was never even mentioned among the human rights cannot be expressed in the categories of the eighteenth century because they presume that rights spring immediately from the "nature" of man—whereby it makes relatively little difference whether this nature is visualized in terms of the natural law or in terms of a being created in the image of God, whether it concerns "natural" rights or divine commands. The decisive factor is that these rights and the human dignity they bestow should remain valid and real even if only a single human being existed on earth; they are independent of human plurality and should remain valid even if a human being is expelled from the human community. . . .

Humanity, which for the eighteenth century, in Kantian terminology, was no more than a regulative idea, has today become an inescapable fact. This new situation, in which "humanity" has in effect assumed the role formerly ascribed to nature or history, would mean in this context that the right to have rights, or the right of every individual to belong to humanity, should be guaranteed by humanity itself. It is by no means certain whether this is possible. For, contrary to the best-intentioned humanitarian attempts to obtain new declarations of human rights from international organizations, it should be understood that this idea transcends the present sphere of international law which still operates in terms of reciprocal agreements and treaties between sovereign states; and, for the time being, a sphere that is above the nations does not exist. Furthermore, this dilemma would by no means be eliminated by the establishment of a "world government." Such a world government is indeed within the realm of possibility, but one may suspect that in reality it might differ considerably from the version promoted by idealistic-minded organizations. The crimes against human rights, which have become a specialty of totalitarian regimes, can always be justified by the pretext that right is equivalent to being good or useful for the whole in distinction to its parts. (Hitler's motto that "Right is what is good for the German people" is only the vulgarized form of a conception of law which can be found everywhere and which in practice will remain ineffectual only so long as older traditions that are still effective in the constitutions prevent this.) A conception of law which identifies what is right with the notion of what is good for—for the individual, or the family, or the people, or the largest number—becomes inevitable once the absolute and transcendent measurements of religion or the law of nature have lost their authority. And this predicament is by no means solved if the unit to which the "good for" applies is as large as mankind itself. For it is quite conceivable, and even within the realm of practical political possibilities, that one fine day a highly organized and mechanized humanity will conclude quite democratically—namely by majority decision—that for humanity as a whole it would be better to liquidate certain parts thereof. Here, in the problems of factual reality, we are confronted with one of the oldest perplexities of political philosophy, which could remain undetected only so long as a stable Christian theology provided the framework for all political and philosophical problems, but which long ago caused Plato to say: "Not man, but a god, must be the measure of all things."

These facts and reflections offer what seems an ironical, bitter, and belated confirmation of the famous arguments with which Edmund Burke opposed the French Revolution's Declaration of the Rights of Man. They appear to buttress his assertion that human rights were an "abstraction," that it was much wiser to rely on an "entailed inheritance" of rights which one transmits to one's children like life itself, and to claim one's rights to be the "rights of an Englishman" rather than the inalienable rights of man. According to Burke, the rights which we enjoy spring "from within the nation," so that neither natural law, nor divine command, nor any concept of mankind such as Robespierre's "human race," "the sovereign of the earth," are needed as a source of law.

The pragmatic soundness of Burke's concept seems to be beyond doubt in the light of our manifold experiences. Not only did loss of national rights in all instances entail the loss of human rights; the restoration of human rights, as the recent example of the State of Israel proves, has been achieved so far only through the restoration or the establishment of national rights. The conception of human rights, based upon the assumed existence of a human being as such, broke down at the very moment when those who professed to believe in it were for the first time confronted with people who had indeed lost all other qualities and specific relationships—except that they were still human. The world found nothing sacred in the abstract nakedness of being human. And in view of objective political conditions, it is hard to say how the concepts of man upon which human rights are based—that he is created in the image of God (in the American formula), or that he is the representative of mankind, or that he harbors within himself the sacred demands of natural law (in the French formula)—could have helped to find a solution to the problem.

The survivors of the extermination camps, the inmates of concentration and internment camps, and even the comparatively happy stateless people could see without Burke's arguments that the abstract nakedness of being nothing but human was their greatest danger. Because of it they were regarded as savages and, afraid that they might end by being considered beasts, they insisted on their nationality, the last sign of their former citizenship, as their only remaining and recognized tie with humanity. Their distrust of natural, their preference for national, rights comes precisely from their realization that natural rights are granted even to savages. Burke had already feared that natural "inalienable" rights would confirm only the "right of the naked savage," and therefore reduce civilized nations to the status of savagery. Because only savages have nothing more to fall back upon than the minimum fact of their human origin, people cling to their nationality all the more desperately when they have lost the rights and protection that such nationality once gave them. Only their past with its "entailed inheritance" seems to attest to the fact that they still belong to the civilized world.

If a human being loses his political status, he should, according to the implications of the inborn and inalienable rights of man, come under exactly the situation for which the declarations of such general rights provided. Actually the opposite is the case. It seems that a man who is nothing but a man has lost the very qualities which make it possible for other people to treat him as a fellow man. This is one of the reasons why it is far more difficult to destroy the legal personality of a criminal, that is of a man who has taken upon himself the responsibility for an act whose consequences now determine his fate, than of a man who has been disallowed all common human responsibilities. . . .

The public sphere is as consistently based on the law of equality as the private sphere is based on the law of universal difference and differentiation. Equality, in contrast to all that is involved in mere existence, is not given us, but is the result of human organization insofar as it is guided by the principle of justice. We are not born equal; we become equal as members of a group on the strength of our decision to guarantee ourselves mutually equal rights.

Our political life rests on the assumption that we can produce equality through organization, because man can act in and change and build a common world, together with his equals and only with his equals. The dark background of mere givenness, the background formed by our unchangeable and unique nature, breaks into the political scene as the alien which in its all too obvious difference reminds us of the limitations of human activity which are identical with the limitations of human equality. The reason why highly developed political communities, such as the ancient city-states or modern nation-states, so often insist on ethnic homogeneity is that they hope to eliminate as far as possible those natural and always present differences and differentiations which by themselves arouse dumb hatred, mistrust, and discrimination because they indicate all too clearly those spheres where men cannot act and change at will, i.e., the limitations of the human artifice. The "alien" is a frightening symbol of the fact of difference as such, of individuality as such, and indicates those realms in which man cannot change and cannot act and in which, therefore, he has a distinct tendency to destroy. If a Negro in a white community is considered a Negro and nothing else, he loses along with his right to equality that freedom of action which is specifically human; all his deeds are now explained as "necessary" consequences of some "Negro" qualities; he has become some specimen of an animal species, called man. Much the same thing happens to those who have lost all distinctive political qualities and have become human beings and nothing else. No doubt, wherever public life and its law of equality are completely victorious, wherever a civilization succeeds in eliminating or reducing to a minimum the dark background of difference, it will end in complete petrifaction and be punished, so to speak, for having forgotten that man is only the master, not the creator of the world.

The great danger arising from the existence of people forced to live outside the common world is that they are thrown back, in the midst of civilization, on their natural givenness, on their mere differentiation. They lack that tremendous equalizing of differences which comes from being citizens of some commonwealth and yet, since they are no longer allowed to partake in the human artifice, they begin to belong to the human race in much the same way as animals belong to a specific animal species. The paradox involved in the loss of human rights is that such loss coincides with the instant when a person becomes a human being in general—without a profession, without a citizenship, without an opinion, without a deed by which to identify and specify himself—*and* different in general, representing nothing but his own absolutely unique individuality which, deprived of expression within and action upon a common world, loses all significance.

The danger in the existence of such people is twofold: first and more obviously, their ever-increasing numbers threaten our political life, our human artifice, the world which is the result of our common and coordinated effort in much the same, perhaps even more terrifying, way as the wild elements of nature once threatened the existence of man-made cities and countrysides. Deadly danger to any civilization is no longer likely to come from without. Nature has been mastered and no barbarians threaten to destroy what they cannot understand, as the Mongolians threatened Europe for centuries. Even the emergence of totalitarian governments is a phenomenon within, not outside, our civilization. The danger is that a global, universally interrelated civilization may produce barbarians from its own midst by forcing millions of people into conditions which, despite all appearances, are the conditions of savages.

—1951

1. How, according to Arendt, is the "whole question of human rights. . . . inextricably blended with the question of national emancipation"?

2. What does Arendt see as the failure of the Rights of Man?

3. What is "one of the oldest perplexities of political philosophy" that caused Plato to say, "Not man, but a god, must be the measure of all things"?

4. Why does Arendt believe that a civilization that succeeds in eliminating the "dark background of difference" will end in "complete petrifaction"?

Crimes of War, Crimes of Peace
by Catharine A. MacKinnon
(selection)

Where, after all, do universal human rights begin? In small places, close to home. . . .

—Eleanor Roosevelt

IN REALITY BEGINS PRINCIPLE. The loftiest legal abstractions, however strenuously empty of social specificity on the surface, are born of social life: amid the intercourse of particular groups, in the presumptive ease of the deciding classes, through the trauma of specific atrocities, at the expense of the silent and excluded, as a victory (usually compromised, often pyrrhic) for the powerless. Law does not grow by syllogistic compulsion; it is pushed by the social logic of domination and challenge to domination, forged in the interaction of change and resistance to change. It is not only in the common law that the life of the law is experience, not logic. Behind all law is someone's story—someone whose blood, if you read closely, leaks through the lines. Text does not beget text; life does. The question—a question of politics and history and therefore law—is whose experience grounds what law.

Human rights principles are based on experience, but not that of women. It is not that women's human rights have not been violated. When women are violated like men who are otherwise like them—when women's arms and legs bleed when severed, when women are shot in pits and gassed in vans, when women's bodies are hidden at the bottom of abandoned mines, when women's skulls are sent from Auschwitz to Strasbourg for experiments—this is not recorded as the history of human rights atrocities to women. They are Argentinian or Honduran or Jewish. When things happen to women that also happen to men, like being beaten and disappeared and tortured to death, the fact that they happened to women is not counted in, or marked as, human suffering. When no war has been declared and still women are beaten by men with whom they are close, when wives disappear from supermarket parking lots, when prostitutes float up in rivers or turn up under piles of rags in abandoned buildings, this is overlooked entirely in the record of human suffering because the victims are women and it smells of sex. What happens to women is either too particular to be universal or too universal to be particular, meaning either too human to be female or too female to be human.

Women are violated in many ways that men are not, or rarely are; many of these violations are sexual and reproductive. Ranging from objectification to killing, from dehumanization and defilement to mutilation and torture to sexual murder, this abuse occurs in forms and settings and legal postures that overlap every recognized human rights convention but is addressed, effectively and as such, by none. What most often happens to women escapes the human rights net. Something—jurisdictional, evidentiary, substantive, customary, or habitual—is always wrong with it. Abuses of women as women rarely seem to fit what these laws and their enforcing bodies have in mind; the more abuses there are, the more they do not fit. Whether in war or in what is called peacetime, at home or abroad, in private or in public, by our side or the other side, man's inhumanity to woman is ignored.

Women's absence shapes human rights in substance and in form, effectively defining what a human and a right are. What does it mean to recognize a principle called human rights that does not really apply to the systemic and systematic violations of the dignity and integrity and security and life of over half the human race? It means that what violates the dignity of others is dignity for them; what violates the integrity of others is integrity for them; what violates the security of others is as much security as they are going to get. Even death to a full human being is less serious for them. Half of humanity is thus effectively defined as nonhuman, subhuman, properly rightsless creatures, beings whose reality of violation, to the extent it is somehow female, floats beneath international legal space.

For a compressed illustration of some current realities that are at once a hair's breadth and a gendered light-year away from the atrocities that ground human rights principles and fill the factual reports of Amnesty International, consider this communication from an American researcher of Bosnian and Croatian descent gathering information in Croatia and Bosnia-Herzegovina:

> Serbian forces have exterminated over 200,000 Croatians and Muslims thus far in an operation they've coined "ethnic cleansing." In this genocide, in Bosnia-Herzegovina alone over 30,000 Muslim and Croatian girls and women are pregnant from mass rape. Of the 100 Serbian-run concentration camps, about 20 are solely rape/death camps for Muslim and Croatian women and children. . . . [There are] news reports and pictures here of Serbian tanks plastered with pornography . . . [and reports that those who] catch the eye of the men looking at the pornography are killed. . . . Some massacres in villages as well as rapes and/or executions in camps are being videotaped as they're happening. One Croatian woman described being tortured by electric shocks and gang-raped in a camp by Serbian men dressed in Croatian uniforms who filmed the rapes and forced her to "confess" on film that Croatians raped her. In the streets of Zagreb, UN troops often ask local women how much they cost. . . . There are reports of refugee women being forced to sexually service them to receive aid. . . . Tomorrow I talk to two survivors of mass rape, thirty men per day for over three months. . . . The UN passed a resolution to collect evidence, a first step for a war crimes trial, but it is said there is no precedent for trying sexual atrocities.

Human rights were born in a cauldron, but it was not this one. Rape, forced motherhood, prostitution, pornography, and sexual murder, on the basis of sex and ethnicity together, have not been the horrors which so "outraged the conscience" [UDHR, Preamble] of the relevant legal world as to imprint themselves on the international legal order.

Formally illegal or not, as policy or merely as what is systematically done, practices of sexual and reproductive abuse occur not only in wartime but also on a daily basis in one form or another in every country in the world. Under domestic and international law, whether or not prohibited on their face, these practices are widely permitted as the liberties of their perpetrators, understood as excesses of passion or spoils of victory, legally rationalized or officially winked at or formally condoned. Even where international instruments could be interpreted to prohibit such practices, it is telling that their cultural supports are more likely to provide the basis for exempting states from their reach than the foundation for a claim of sex discrimination.

The war against Croatia and Bosnia-Herzegovina exemplifies how existing approaches to human rights can work to cover up and confuse who is doing what to whom and effectively condone atrocities. All state parties are apparently covered by most of the relevant international human rights guarantees and laws of war, certainly by customary international law. But nothing has yet been invoked to stop the abuses described in the communication or to hold the perpetrators accountable. What is the problem? The fact of Serbian aggression is beyond question, just as the fact of male aggression against women is beyond question, here and everywhere. "Ethnic cleansing" is a Serbian policy of extermination of non-Serbs with the goal of "all Serbs in one nation," a "Greater Serbia" encompassing what was called Yugoslavia. "Ethnic cleansing" is a euphemism for genocide. Yet this genocidal war of aggression has repeatedly been construed as bilateral, a civil war or an ethnic conflict, to the accompaniment of much international wonderment that people cannot get along and pious clucking at the behavior of "all sides" in a manner reminiscent of blaming women for getting themselves raped by men they know. To call this a civil war is like calling the Holocaust a civil war between German Aryans and German Jews.

One result of this equalization of aggressor with aggressedagainst is that these rapes are not grasped either as a strategy in genocide or as a practice of misogyny, far less as both at once, continuous at once with *this* ethnic war of aggression and with *the* gendered war of aggression of everyday life. This war is to everyday rape what the Holocaust was to everyday anti-Semitism. Muslim and Croatian women and girls are raped, then murdered, by Serbian military men, regulars and irregulars, in their homes, in rape/death camps, on hillsides, everywhere. Their corpses are often raped as well. When this is noticed, it is either as genocide or as rape, or as femicide but not genocide, but not as rape as a form of genocide directed specifically at women. It is seen either as part of a campaign of Serbia against non-Serbia or an onslaught by combatants against civilians, but not an attack by men against women. Or, in the feminist whitewash, it becomes just another instance of aggression by all men against all women all the time, rather than what it is, which is rape by certain men against certain women. The point seems to be to obscure, by any means available, exactly who is doing what to whom and why.

When the women survive, the rapes tend to be regarded as an inevitability of armed conflict, part of the war of all against all, or as a continuation of the hostilities of civil life, of all men against all women. Rape *does* occur in war among and between all sides; rape is a daily act by men against women and is always an act of domination by men over women. But the fact that these rapes are part of an ethnic war of extermination, being misrepresented as a civil war among equal aggressors, means that Muslim and Croatian women are facing twice as many rapists with twice as many excuses, two layers of men on top of them rather than one, and two layers of impunity serving to justify the rapes: just war and just life.

Like all rapes, these rapes are particular as well as generic, and the particularity matters. This is ethnic rape as an official policy of war: not only a policy of the pleasure of male power unleashed; not only a policy to defile, torture, humiliate, degrade, and demoralize the other side; not only a policy of men posturing to gain advantage and ground over other men. It is rape under orders: not out of control, under control. It is rape unto death, rape as massacre, rape to kill or make the victims wish they were dead. It is rape as an instrument of forced exile, to make you leave your home and never come back. It is rape to be seen and heard by others, rape as spectacle. It is rape to shatter a people, to drive a wedge through a community. It is the rape of misogyny liberated by xenophobia and unleashed by official command.

It is rape made sexy for the perpetrators by the defenselessness and youth of many of the victims and the rapists' absolute power to select victims at will. It is rape made more arousing by ethnic hostility against a designated enemy—"For Serbia"—and made to seem right by lies about the behavior of that enemy. It is rape made exciting by knowing that there are no limits on what can be done, that the women *can* be raped to death. Most of all, it is rape made sexually irresistible by the fact that the women *are* about to be sacrificed, by the ultimate power of reducing a person to a corpse, by the powerlessness of the women and children in the face of their imminent murder at the hands of their rapist. It is murder as the ultimate sexual act. Do not say it is not sex for the men. When the men are told to take the women away and not bring them back, they rape them, *then* kill them, then sometimes rape them again, cut off their breasts, and rip out their wombs. One woman was allowed to live so long as she kept her Serbian captor hard all night orally, night after night after night.

This is rape as torture and rape as extermination. Some women who are not killed speak of wanting to take their own lives. It is at once mass rape and serial rape indistinguishable from prostitution. It is concentration camp as brothel: women impounded to be passed around by men among men. It is also rape as a policy of ethnic uniformity and ethnic conquest, annexation and expansion, acquisition by one nation of others, colonization of women's bodies as colonization of the culture they symbolize and embody as well as of the territory they occupy. It is rape because a Serb wants your apartment. Most distinctively, it is rape for reproduction *as* ethnic liquidation: Croatian and Muslim women are raped to help make a Serbian state by making Serbian babies.

This is ethnic rape. If this were racial rape, it would be pure pollution, the children regarded as dirty and contaminated: their mothers' babies, as in the American South under slavery, Black babies. Because it is ethnic rape, the children are regarded as clean and purified: their fathers' babies, Serbian babies, as clean as anyone with a woman's blood in them and on them can be. The idea seems to be to create a fifth column within Croatian and Muslim society, children (all sons?) who will rise up and join their fathers. Much Serbian ideology and practice takes a page from the Nazi book. Combining with it the archaic view that the sperm carries all the genetic material, the Serbs have achieved the ultimate racialization of culture, the (one hopes) final conclusion of Nazism: now culture is genetic.

The spectacle of the United Nations troops violating the population they are supposed to protect adds a touch of the perverse. My correspondent observes that "there are . . . reports of UN troops participating in raping Muslim and Croatian women from the Serb rape/death camps. Their presence has apparently increased trafficking in women and girls through the opening of brothels, brothel-massage parlors, peep shows, and the local production of pornographic films." A former United Nations Protection Force (Unprofor) commander reportedly accepted offers from Serbian commanders to bring him Muslim girls from the camps for orgies. This paradigmatic instance of the male bond across official lines pointedly poses, in the gender context, Juvenal's question of who shall guard the guardians—especially when the guardians are already there to guard the other guardians. The Nazis took pictures, but in its sophisticated employment of media technology, in the openness of its use of pornography, in its conscious making of pornography of its atrocities, this is perhaps the first truly modern war.

Where do international human rights and humanitarian law stand on this? In real terms, the rules that govern the law's treatment of women elsewhere pertain here as well: A human is not one who is sexually and reproductively violated. One is not human "down there." Nor is a human right something a man in society or in a state of nature takes away from you and others like you. In fact, there are no others like you, because "a man" defines what "an individual" means, and human rights are mostly "individual" rights. Men have their human rights violated; rather, when someone's human rights are recognized as violated, he is probably a man. Men are permitted to be individuals, so can be violated as individuals. If you are hurt as a member of a group, the odds that the group will be considered human are improved if it includes men. Under guarantees of international human rights, as well as in everyday life, a woman is "not yet a name for a way of being human."

A right, as this legal definition is lived in reality, becomes something no woman, as a member of the group women, has to lose. A right is also something only an entity with the power of a nation can violate; it is a duty of government not to interfere with civil and political liberties as they socially exist. The role of international law has been largely, in Isaiah Berlin's sense, negative. It could be more, but it fosters human rights less through mandating governmental intervention than through enforcing governmental abstinence. In other words, if your human rights are going to be violated, pray it is by someone who looks like a government, and that he already acted, and acted wrong. . . .

Male reality has become human rights principle, or at least the principle governing human rights practice. Men have and take liberties as a function of their social power as men. Men have often needed state force to get away with subjecting other men; slavery, segregation in the United States, and Hitler's persecutions were explicitly legalized. So the model of human rights violation is based on state action. The result is, when men use their liberties socially to deprive women of theirs, it does not look like a human rights violation. But when men are deprived of theirs by governments, it does. The violations of the human rights of men better fit the paradigm of human rights violations because that paradigm has been based on the experiences of men.

In the case of women, by contrast, because male dominance is built into the social structure, social force is often enough.

States collaborate elaborately, not just by abdicating social life but by intervening legally to entitle men to much of the power they socially exercise, legitimating what men can get away with in fact. Even recognizing active state involvement, most women are not directly raped, forcibly impregnated, and trafficked by state policy, at least not most of the time. Although the state in some way stands behind most of what men do to women, men typically have enough power to control and violate women without the state explicitly intervening to allow it. To this extent, women are not seen as subjected by the state as such, so their condition is regarded as prelegal, social hence natural, so outside international human rights accountability.

Now consider that most human rights instruments empower states to act against states, rather than individuals or groups to act on their own behalf. Given that only state violations of human rights are recognized, this is very odd. States are the only ones recognized as violating human rights, yet states are also the only ones empowered to redress them. Not only are men's so-called "private" acts against women left out; power to act against public acts are left exclusively in the hands of those who commit those acts. No state effectively guarantees women's human rights within its borders. No state has an incentive to break ranks by setting a human rights standard for women's status and treatment that no state yet meets. Internationally, men's states protect each other the way men protect each other from accountability for violations of women within states. At least this is one explanation for the failure of international human rights law effectively to empower individuals or groups of women to enforce their own human rights against individuals and states alike. Which state is in a position to challenge another state on women's human rights? Which state ever will?

Wartime is largely exceptional in that atrocities by soldiers against civilians are always state acts. But men do in war what they do in peace, only more so. When it comes to women, at least to civilian casualties, the complacency that surrounds peacetime extends to war, however the laws read. And the more a conflict can be framed as *within* a state, as a civil war, as social, as domestic, the less human rights are recognized as being violated. In other words, the closer a fight comes to home, the more "feminized" the victims become no matter what their gender, and the less likely international human rights will be found to be violated, no matter what was done.

The received concepts at work here have a complex history, mostly a Western one, which can be read and compressed as follows. The contractarian liberals, building on Greek and Roman antecedents, opposed medieval status notions that assigned human value within a rigid hierarchy based on birth. Seeking to secure human freedom against state tyranny, they posited the radical notion that each person, qua human, had, meaning had by nature, irrevocable and equal entitlements to life, liberty, security, dignity, property, and so on. Through the American and French revolutions, this idea of inalienable human worth called individual rights was entrenched, checking organized power in the form of government. Subsequently, some transnational agreements further elevated and enshrined the same recognitions as binding among state parties.

Then the Third Reich utterly violated all such rights . . . isolating and then liquidating those it saw as inferior or polluting or oppositional. In particular, the official attempted extermination of the Jews as a people galvanized the notion of supranational guarantees of human rights with a survival urgency. This organized genocide by government policy indelibly marked and fundamentally shaped the content, priorities, sensitivities, and deep structure of the received law of human rights in our time. In a reading of this reality, more than any other, contemporary human rights finds its principled ground.

Largely beneath notice in this tradition has been the status of women as such, socially subordinated to men and excluded or ignored, marginalized or subjected by state policy. Women's enforced inequality has been a reality on which all these systems are materially predicated, so seamlessly it has been invisible. Women were not citizens in Greek democracy; they were wives, slaves, prostitutes. In this setting, Aristotle formulated his equality principle as treating likes alike and unlikes unalike—a concept fundamentally unquestioned since, including in the international human rights context. In this approach, it does not matter whether one is hurt or helped, permitted to dominate or kept subordinated; all that matters is that empirical condition, no matter how created, fits normative treatment. That women were apparently so different to Aristotle as not to be treated unequally under his principle when excluded from citizenship has not been considered a drawback or an indication that something is amiss.

Building on this tradition, the original liberals formulated their social compacts in and for societies in which women could not even vote. With the exception of John Stuart Mill, they did not see a problem in this, projecting their purportedly universal notions of what have come to be called human rights in ways that did not explicitly include women and effectively kept most women from access to them. Humans own property; women mostly cannot; more often they are property. Humans are equal because they can kill; women are socialized not to kill and are punished, not glorified, when they do. Humans consent to a regime or leave it; women have no voice to dissent, no place to go, and no means of leaving. At the same time, guarantees women specifically need, due to sex inequality in society, in order to live to a standard defined as human—like freedom from being bought and sold as sexual chattel, autonomous economic means, reproductive control, personal security from intimate invasion, a credible voice in public life, a nonderivative place in the world—were not considered at all.

What women need for equality was not only not guaranteed; much of women's inequality was guaranteed in the form of men's individual civil liberties. In these theories, abuses of women were tacitly if not explicitly condoned as individual rights. What were called individual rights have become, in life, rights of men as a group over women individually and as a class. Women's rape becomes men's liberty, gang rape their fraternity, prostitution their property, forced pregnancy their family and their privacy, pornography their speech. Put another way, whatever their rebellions accomplished for human freedom, and it was substantial, the American Revolution did not free the slaves, and the French Revolution did free the Marquis de Sade—facts connected by legitimating a traffic in human beings and the sexual abuse of women for economic gain. Understand: This is what the received concept of equality meant and largely still means.

Because women are a group whose claim to human status is tenuous and denied, the attempt to apply human rights law to women as such makes two more general problems worse. Human rights have no ground and no teeth. As to teeth, human rights are enforced internationally primarily between states, states that agree to them. Many, such as the United States, do not agree to many of them. Enforcement is mainly through reporting, meaning moral force, meaning effective nonenforcement. Signatory countries are even permitted formal excuse from compliance, a practice disproportionately used to evade sex equality provisions. The covenants against trafficking in women, for example, are many and venerable, yet the traffic continues unabated, untouched, flourishing. Thailand even traffics in women by policy. China may officially force abortions and sterilizations, yet nothing is done. Enforcement of human rights against states' lack of action and against private parties may be possible in principle but is virtually absent in practice. For women, international human rights presents the biggest gap between principle and practice in the known legal world.

Many existing international instruments guarantee sex equality. Yet so little of women's experience of violation of human rights has been brought under them that it becomes necessary to inquire into the foundations of human rights to explain why. The primary foundation of human rights has been natural law, a secular religion that moves only those who believe in it. Its content tends to redescribe the social status quo and attribute it to nature. (Emphatic use of the existential verb to affirm loudly and often that women "are" human beings carries only the clout of its speaker's decibel level.) Positive law helps little more, since women have had little voice in its formulation in most places. Morality, an alternative ground, can be moving, but does not mean anyone has to do anything, as illustrated by the use of the phrase "moral victory" to refer to an actual defeat. All these grounds come down to social power in the end. If you have it, you can meet their tests for "human"; but power is exactly what women are socially denied, which is why their human rights can be violated and why they need them recognized.

At its philosophical foundations, the natural law tradition on which human rights remain primarily based has never been clear on whether women are men's natural equals. Rather, to oversimplify a complicated debate, it has been relatively clear that they are not, and has provided no method for resolving different conclusions, each equally firmly said to be predicated on the law of nature. Nor has it reconciled its observation that sex is a natural difference with its view that equality is predicated on natural identity. To those who ground human rights in the opportunity to live out one's life project rationally, it should be pointed out that, socially speaking, women as women have not been permitted a life project and are widely considered as not possessed of rationality, or of what passes for reason among men. Others ground human rights in basic personal liberty or in fundamental human dignity, the problem being that you already have to have them to have a human right violated when you are denied them. So, it's back to nature.

Mortimer Adler exemplifies rather than exposes this circularity: "If there are no natural rights, there are no human rights; if there are no human rights, there cannot be any crimes against humanity." Women's problem has been that society and law do not agree that nature made them human, so nothing that is done to them is a crime against humanity, because they have none. If society gives you no rights, such that a state need never deny them to keep you from having them, it may do you little good to have them formally guaranteed in international law. Free of this essentialist circularity, the task is to ground a claim to crimes against humanity clear of natural rights, which are not recognized to exist in nature unless they are recognized to exist in society. In other words, all discourse about nature is a social discourse.

Horror at the Holocaust grounds modern morality. No one knows what is good, but nearly everyone knows the Holocaust was evil. We may not know what human is, but the Holocaust was inhuman. Jewish women were distinctively abused in ways that connect to anti-Semitic misogyny to this day and startlingly resemble the tortures of Croatian and Muslim women by Serbs. The horrific tortures and extermination of millions of Jews of both sexes because they were Jews has overshadowed everything then and since.

Considered in terms of equality theory, the Third Reich can be seen to follow an unbroken line from Aristotle through American segregation of treating "likes alike and unlikes unalike"—Jews having been rendered "unlike" Aryans. Yet human rights law still uses the same equality concept, without reassessment. The dominant lesson that seems to have been learned is that Jews could be and were annihilated because they were "different," not that something is wrong with an equality standard that permits extermination for "differences." The Jews failed the equality test—not the equality test failed the Jews. Not that a better equality theory would have stopped Hitler. But what is one to make of an equality principle apparently logically consistent with, and undisturbed by, genocide? If equality's abstractions are so receptive to Nazi substance, are they perhaps a flawed vehicle for social justice? The fact that international law pervasively guarantees sex equality, yet there is no sex equality, while mass rape and forced childbearing go on both in peacetime and in war, including in genocidal war, suddenly begins to make sense.

—1993

114

1. Why does MacKinnon claim that human rights principles are not based on the experience of women?

2. According to MacKinnon, why is "man's inhumanity to woman" ignored?

3. What does MacKinnon mean when she says, "What happens to women is either too particular to be universal or too universal to be particular, meaning either too human to be female or too female to be human"?

4. Why does MacKinnon compare the war in Bosnia to the Holocaust?

5. What does MacKinnon mean when she says that in Bosnia there are "two layers of impunity serving to justify the rapes: just war and just life"?

6. How, according to MacKinnon, is the presently formulated "equality principle . . . logically consistent with, and undisturbed by, genocide"?

Human Rights, Rationality, and Sentimentality
by Richard Rorty

(selection)

PLATO ARGUED THAT THERE IS A BIG DIFFERENCE between us and the animals, a difference worthy of respect and cultivation. He thought that human beings have a special added ingredient which puts them in a different ontological category than the brutes. Respect for this ingredient provides a reason for people to be nice to each other. Anti-Platonists like Nietzsche reply that attempts to get people to stop murdering, raping, and castrating each other are, in the long run, doomed to fail—for the real truth about human nature is that we are a uniquely nasty and dangerous kind of animal. When contemporary admirers of Plato claim that all featherless bipeds—even the stupid and childlike, even the women, even the sodomized—have the same inalienable rights, admirers of Nietzsche reply that the very idea of "inalienable human rights" is, like the idea of a special added ingredient, a laughably feeble attempt by the weaker members of the species to fend off the stronger.

As I see it, one important intellectual advance made in our century is the steady decline in interest in the quarrel between Plato and Nietzsche. There is a growing willingness to neglect the question "What is our nature?" and to substitute the question "What can we make of ourselves?" We are much less inclined than our ancestors were to take "theories of human nature" seriously, much less inclined to take ontology or history as a guide to life. We have come to see that the only lesson of either history or anthropology is our extraordinary malleability. We are coming to think of ourselves as the flexible, protean, self-shaping animal rather than as the rational animal or the cruel animal.

One of the shapes we have recently assumed is that of a human rights culture. I borrow the term "human rights culture" from the Argentinian jurist and philosopher Eduardo Rabossi. In an article called "Human Rights Naturalized," Rabossi argues that philosophers should think of this culture as a new, welcome fact of the post-Holocaust world. They should stop trying to get behind or beneath this fact, stop trying to detect and defend its so-called "philosophical presuppositions." On Rabossi's view, philosophers like Alan Gewirth are wrong to argue that human rights cannot depend on historical facts. "My basic point," Rabossi says, is that "the world has changed, that the human rights phenomenon renders human rights foundationalism outmoded and irrelevant."

Rabossi's claim that human rights foundationalism is *outmoded* seems to me both true and important; it will be my principal topic in this lecture. I shall be enlarging on, and defending, Rabossi's claim that the question whether human beings really have the rights enumerated in the Helsinki Declaration [Conference on Security and Cooperation in Europe, 1975] is not worth raising. In particular, I shall be defending the claim that nothing relevant to moral choice separates human beings from animals except historically contingent facts of the world, cultural facts.

This claim is sometimes called "cultural relativism" by those who indignantly reject it. One reason they reject it is that such relativism seems to them incompatible with the fact that our human rights culture, the culture with which we in this democracy identify ourselves, is morally superior to other cultures. I quite agree that ours is morally superior, but I do not think this superiority counts in favor of the existence of a universal human nature. It would only do so if we assumed that a moral claim is ill-founded if not backed up by knowledge of a distinctively human attribute. But it is not clear why "respect for human dignity"—our sense that the differences between Serb and Muslim, Christian and infidel, gay and straight, male and female should not matter—must presuppose the existence of any such attribute.

Traditionally, the name of the shared human attribute which supposedly "grounds" morality is "rationality." Cultural relativism is associated with irrationalism because it denies the existence of morally relevant transcultural facts. To agree with Rabossi one must, indeed, be irrationalist in that sense. But one need not be irrationalist in the sense of ceasing to make one's web of belief as coherent, and as perspicuously structured, as possible. Philosophers like myself, who think of rationality as simply the attempt at such coherence, agree with Rabossi that foundationalist projects are outmoded. We see our task as a matter of making our own culture—the human rights culture—more self-conscious and more powerful, rather than of demonstrating its superiority to other cultures by an appeal to something transcultural.

We think that the most philosophy can hope to do is summarize our culturally influenced intuitions about the right thing to do in various situations. The summary is effected by formulating a generalization from which these intuitions can be deduced, with the help of noncontroversial lemmas. That generalization is not supposed to ground our intuitions, but rather to summarize them. John Rawls's "Difference Principle" and the U.S. Supreme Court's construction, in recent decades, of a constitutional "right to privacy" are examples of this kind of summary. We see the formulation of such summarizing generalizations as increasing the predictability, and thus the power and efficiency, of our institutions, thereby heightening the sense of shared moral identity which brings us together in a moral community.

Foundationalist philosophers, such as Plato, Aquinas, and Kant, have hoped to provide independent support for such summarizing generalizations. They would like to infer these generalizations from further premises, premises capable of being known to be true independently of the truth of the moral intuitions which have been summarized. Such premises are supposed to justify our intuitions, by providing premises from which the content of those intuitions can be deduced. I shall lump all such premises together under the label "claims to knowledge about the nature of human beings." In this broad sense, claims to know that our moral intuitions are recollections of the Form of the Good, or that we are the disobedient children of a loving God, or that human beings differ from other kinds of animals by having dignity rather than mere value, are all claims about human nature. So are such counterclaims as that human beings are merely vehicles for selfish genes, or merely eruptions of the will to power.

To claim such knowledge is to claim to know something which, though not itself a moral intuition, can *correct* moral intuitions. It is essential to this idea of moral knowledge that a whole community might come to know that most of their most salient intuitions about the right thing to do were wrong. But now suppose we ask: *Is* there this sort of knowledge? What kind of question is that? On the traditional view, it is a philosophical question, belonging to a branch of epistemology known as "metaethics." But on the pragmatist view which I favor, it is a question of efficiency, of how best to grab hold of history— how best to bring about the utopia sketched by the Enlightenment. If the activities of those who attempt to achieve this sort of knowledge seem of little use in actualizing this utopia, that is a reason to think there is no such knowledge. . . .

We pragmatists argue from the fact that the emergence of the human rights culture seems to owe nothing to increased moral knowledge, and everything to hearing sad and sentimental stories, to the conclusion that there is probably no knowledge of the sort Plato envisaged. We go on to argue: Since no useful work seems to be done by insisting on a purportedly

119

ahistorical human nature, there probably is no such nature, or at least nothing in that nature that is relevant to our moral choices. . . .

We remain profoundly grateful to philosophers like Plato and Kant, not because they discovered truths but because they prophesied cosmopolitan utopias—utopias most of whose details they may have got wrong, but utopias we might never have struggled to reach had we not heard their prophecies. As long as our ability to know, and in particular to discuss the question "What is man?" seemed the most important thing about us human beings, people like Plato and Kant accompanied utopian prophecies with claims to know something deep and important—something about the parts of the soul, or the transcendental status of the common moral consciousness. But this ability, and those questions, have, in the course of the last two hundred years, come to seem much less important. Rabossi summarizes this cultural sea change in his claim that human rights foundationalism is outmoded. In the remainder of this lecture, I shall take up the questions: *Why* has knowledge become much less important to our self-image than it was two hundred years ago? Why does the attempt to found culture on nature, and moral obligation on knowledge of transcultural universals, seem so much less important to us than it seemed in the Enlightenment? Why is there so little resonance, and so little point, in asking whether human beings in fact have the rights listed in the Helsinki Declaration? Why, in short, has moral philosophy become such an inconspicuous part of our culture?

A simple answer is that between Kant's time and ours Darwin argued most of the intellectuals out of the view that human beings contain a special added ingredient. He convinced most of us that we were exceptionally talented animals, animals clever enough to take charge of our own future evolution. I think this answer is right as far as it goes, but it leads to a further question: Why did Darwin succeed, relatively speaking, so very easily? Why did he not cause the creative philosophical ferment caused by Galileo and Newton? . . .

The best explanation of both Darwin's relatively easy triumph, and our own increasing willingness to substitute hope for knowledge, is that the nineteenth and twentieth centuries saw, among the Europeans and Americans, an extraordinary increase in wealth, literacy, and leisure. This increase made possible an unprecedented acceleration in the rate of moral progress. Such events as the French Revolution and the ending of the transatlantic slave trade prompted nineteenth-century intellectuals in the rich democracies to say: It is enough for us to know that we live in an age in which human beings can make things much better for ourselves. We do not need to dig behind this historical fact to nonhistorical facts about what we really are.

In the two centuries since the French Revolution, we have learned that human beings are far more malleable than Plato or Kant had dreamed. The more we are impressed by this malleability, the less interested we become in questions about our ahistorical nature. The more we see a chance to recreate ourselves, the more we read Darwin not as offering one more theory about what we really are but as providing reasons why we need not ask what we really are. Nowadays, to say that we are clever animals is not to say something philosophical and pessimistic but something political and hopeful, namely: If we can work together, we can make ourselves into whatever we are clever and courageous enough to imagine ourselves becoming. This sets aside Kant's question "What is Man?" and substitutes the question "What sort of world can we prepare for our great-grandchildren?"

The question "What is Man?" in the sense of "What is the deep ahistorical nature of human beings?" owed its popularity to the standard answer to that question: We are the *rational* animal, the one which can know as well as merely feel. The residual popularity of this answer accounts for the residual popularity of Kant's astonishing claim that sentimentality has nothing to do with morality, that there is something distinctively and transculturally human called "the sense of moral obligation" which has nothing to do with love, friendship, trust, or social solidarity. As long as we believe *that*, people like Rabossi are going to have a tough time convincing us that human rights foundationalism is an outmoded project.

To overcome this idea of a *sui generis* sense of moral obligation, it would help to stop answering the question "What makes us different from the other animals?" by saying "We can know, and they can merely feel." We should substitute "We can feel *for each other* to a much greater extent than they can." . . .

The best, and probably the only, argument for putting foundationalism behind us is the one I have already suggested: It would be more efficient to do so, because it would let us concentrate our energies on manipulating sentiments, on sentimental education. That sort of education sufficiently acquaints people of different kinds with one another so that they are less tempted to think of those different from themselves as only quasi-human. The goal of this manipulation of sentiment is to expand the reference of the terms "our kind of people" and "people like us." . . .

By insisting that he could reeducate people who had matured without acquiring appropriate moral sentiments by invoking a higher power than sentiment, the power of reason, Plato got moral philosophy off on the wrong foot. He led moral philosophers to concentrate on the rather rare figure of the psychopath, the person who has no concern for any human being other than himself. Moral philosophy has systematically neglected the much more common case: the person whose treatment of a rather narrow range of featherless bipeds is morally impeccable, but who remains indifferent to the suffering of those outside this range, the ones he or she thinks of as pseudohumans.

Plato set things up so that moral philosophers think they have failed unless they convince the rational egotist that he should not be an egotist—convince him by telling him about his true, unfortunately neglected, self. But the rational egotist is not the problem. The problem is the gallant and honorable Serb who sees Muslims as circumcised dogs. It is the brave soldier and good comrade who loves and is loved by his mates, but who thinks of women as dangerous, malevolent whores and bitches.

Plato thought that the way to get people to be nicer to each other was to point out what they all had in common—rationality. But it does little good to point out, to the people I have just described, that many Muslims and women are good at mathematics or engineering or jurisprudence. Resentful young Nazi toughs were quite aware that many Jews were clever and learned, but this only added to the pleasure they took in beating them up. Nor does it do much good to get such people to read Kant, and agree that one should not treat rational agents simply as means. For everything turns on who counts as a fellow human being, as a rational agent in the only relevant sense—the sense in which rational agency is synonymous with membership in *our* moral community. . . .

Outside the circle of post-Enlightenment European culture, the circle of relatively safe and secure people who have been manipulating each others' sentiments for two hundred years, most people are simply unable to understand why membership in a biological species is supposed to suffice for membership in a moral community. This is not because they are insufficiently rational. It is, typically, because they live in a world in which it would be just too risky—indeed, would often be insanely dangerous—to let one's sense of moral community stretch beyond one's family, clan, or tribe.

To get whites to be nicer to Blacks, males to females, Serbs to Muslims, or straights to gays, to help our species link up into what Rabossi calls a "planetary community" dominated by a culture of human rights, it is of no use whatever to say, with Kant: Notice that what you have in common, your humanity, is more important than these trivial differences. For the people we are trying to convince will rejoin that they notice nothing of the sort. Such people are *morally* offended by the suggestion that they should treat someone who is not kin as if he were a brother, or a nigger as if he were white, or a queer as if he were normal, or an infidel as if she were a believer. They are offended by the suggestion that they treat people whom they do not think of as human as if they were human. . . .

This rejoinder is not just a rhetorical device, nor is it in any way irrational. It is heartfelt. The identity of these people, the people whom we should like to convince to join our Eurocentric human rights culture, is bound up with their sense of who they are *not*. Most people—especially people relatively untouched by the European Enlightenment—simply do not think of themselves as, first and foremost, a human being. Instead, they think of themselves as being a certain *good* sort of human being—a sort defined by explicit opposition to a particularly bad sort. It is crucial for their sense of who they are that they are *not* an infidel, *not* a queer, *not* a woman, *not* an untouchable. Just insofar as they are impoverished, and as their lives are perpetually at risk, they have little else than pride in not being what they are not to sustain their self-respect. Starting with the days when the term "human being" was synonymous with "member of our tribe," we have always thought of human beings in terms of paradigm members of the species. We have contrasted *us*, the *real* humans, with rudimentary, or perverted, or deformed examples of humanity.

We Eurocentric intellectuals like to suggest that we, the paradigm humans, have overcome this primitive parochialism by using that paradigmatic human faculty, reason. So we say that failure to concur with us is due to "prejudice." . . .

[The] bad people are no less rational, no less clearheaded, no more prejudiced, than we good people who respect otherness. The bad people's problem is that they were not so lucky in the circumstances of their upbringing as we were. Instead of treating as irrational all those people out there who are trying to find and kill Salman Rushdie, we should treat them as deprived.

Foundationalists think of these people as deprived of truth, of moral knowledge. But it would be better—more specific, more suggestive of possible remedies—to think of them as deprived of two more concrete things: security and sympathy. By "security" I mean conditions of life sufficiently risk-free as to make one's difference from others inessential to one's self-respect, one's sense of worth. These conditions have been enjoyed by Americans and Europeans—the people who dreamed up the human rights culture—much more than they have been enjoyed by anyone else. By "sympathy" I mean the sort of reaction that the Athenians had more of after seeing Aeschylus' *The Persians* than before, the sort that white Americans had more of after reading *Uncle Tom's Cabin* than before, the sort that we have more of after watching TV programs about the genocide in Bosnia. Security and sympathy go together, for the same reasons that peace and economic productivity go together. The tougher things are, the more you have to be afraid of, the more dangerous your situation, the less you can afford the time or effort to think about what things might be like for people with whom you do not immediately identify. Sentimental education only works on people who can relax long enough to listen.

If Rabossi and I are right in thinking human rights foundationalism outmoded, then Hume is a better advisor than Kant about how we intellectuals can hasten the coming of the Enlightenment utopia for which both men yearned. Among contemporary philosophers, the best advisor seems to me to be Annette Baier. Baier describes Hume as "the woman's moral philosopher" because Hume held that "corrected (sometimes rule-corrected) sympathy, not law-discerning reason, is the fundamental moral capacity." Baier would like us to get rid of both the Platonic idea that we have a true self, and the Kantian idea that it is rational to be moral. In aid of this project, she suggests that we think of "trust" rather than "obligation" as the fundamental moral notion. This substitution would mean thinking of the spread of the human rights culture not as a matter of our becoming more aware of the requirements of the moral law, but rather as what Baier calls "a progress of sentiments." This progress consists in an increasing ability to see the similarities between ourselves and people very unlike us as outweighing the differences. It is the result of what I have been calling "sentimental education." The relevant similarities are not a matter of sharing a deep true self which instantiates true humanity, but are such little, superficial similarities as cherishing our parents and our children—similarities that do not interestingly distinguish us from many nonhuman animals. . . .

If one follows Baier's advice one will not see it as the moral educator's task to answer the rational egotist's question "Why should I be moral?" but rather to answer the much more frequently posed question "Why should I care about a stranger, a person who is no kin to me, a person whose habits I find disgusting?" The traditional answer to the latter question is "Because kinship and custom are morally irrelevant, irrelevant to the obligations imposed by the recognition of membership in the same species." This has never been very convincing, since it begs the question at issue: whether mere species membership is, in fact, a sufficient surrogate for closer kinship. Furthermore, that answer leaves one wide open to Nietzsche's discomfiting rejoinder: *That* universalistic notion, Nietzsche will sneer, would only have crossed the mind of a slave—or, perhaps, the mind of an intellectual, a priest whose self-esteem and livelihood both depend on getting the rest of us to accept a sacred, unarguable, unchallengeable paradox.

A better sort of answer is the sort of long, sad, sentimental story which begins "Because this is what it is like to be in her situation—to be far from home, among strangers," or "Because she might become your daughter-in-law," or "Because her mother would grieve for her." Such stories, repeated and varied over the centuries, have induced us, the rich, safe, powerful people, to tolerate, and even to cherish, powerless people—people whose appearance or habits or beliefs at first seemed an insult to our own moral identity, our sense of the limits of permissible human variation. . . .

These [last] two centuries are most easily understood not as a period of deepening understanding of the nature of rationality or of morality, but rather as one in which there occurred an astonishingly rapid progress of sentiments, in which it has become much easier for us to be moved to action by sad and sentimental stories.

This progress has brought us to a moment in human history in which it is plausible for Rabossi to say that the human rights phenomenon is a "fact of the world." This phenomenon may be just a blip. But it may mark the beginning of a time in which gang rape brings forth as strong a response when it happens to women as when it happens to men, or when it happens to foreigners as when it happens to people like us.

—*1993*

126

1. Why does Rorty see the decline in interest about theories of human nature as an "intellectual advance"?

2. Why does Rorty argue against "the existence of a universal human nature"?

3. Why is Rorty confident that sentiment as a vehicle of education will lead to moral progress?

4. Why does Rorty think we should "concentrate our energies on manipulating sentiments" to expand the human rights culture and not some other culture?

5. Why is Rorty confident that "our human rights culture" is "morally superior"?

6. Why does Rorty want us to use sympathy instead of reason and rationality to extend the human rights culture?

Acknowledgments

The Great Books Foundation wishes to thank the following authors, publishers and representatives for permission to reprint copyrighted material.

Declaration of the Rights of Man and the Citizen, from THE COMING OF THE FRENCH REVOLUTION, by Georges Lefebvre. Translated by R. R. Palmer. Copyright 1947 by Princeton University Press. Reprinted by permission of Princeton University Press.

The Perplexities of the Rights of Man, from THE ORIGINS OF TOTALITARIANISM, by Hannah Arendt. Copyright 1951, and renewed 1979 by Mary McCarthy West. Reprinted by permission of Harcourt Brace & Company.

Crimes of War, Crimes of Peace, by Catharine A. MacKinnon, from ON HUMAN RIGHTS: OXFORD AMNESTY LECTURES 1993, edited by Stephen Shute and Susan Hurley. Copyright 1993 by Basic Books, Inc. Reprinted by permission of BasicBooks, a subsidiary of Perseus Books Group, LLC.

Human Rights, Rationality, and Sentimentality, by Richard Rorty, from ON HUMAN RIGHTS: OXFORD AMNESTY LECTURES 1993, edited by Stephen Shute and Susan Hurley. Copyright 1993 by Basic Books, Inc. Reprinted by permission of BasicBooks, a subsidiary of Perseus Books Group, LLC.

The Great Books Foundation also wishes to thank the following people and institutions for their help in selecting and evaluating readings and in formulating discussion questions for this volume:

The regional Great Books councils; the Humanities and Sciences Institute in Phoenix, Arizona; the Franklin and Eleanor Roosevelt Institute; the Chicago *And Justice for All* test group; and the numerous Great Books Foundation staff members who took a special interest in this project.